AF082011

THE SURVIVAL CEO BLUEPRINT

A STEP-BY-STEP REPEATABLE SYSTEM FOR BUILDING A BUSINESS AROUND WHAT YOU LOVE TO DO

CREEK STEWART

DROPSToNE PRESS
The Survival CEO Blueprint
Creek Stewart

Copyright © 2020 by Creek Stewart

All Rights Reserved

Copy editor: Jacob Perry

All rights reserved. No part of this book may be reproduced in any form by any means without express permission of the author. This includes reprints, excerpts, photocopying, recording or any future means of reproducing text.

If you would like to do any of the above, please seek permission first by contacting us at http://www.dropstonepress.com

Wholesale inquiries please visit http://www.dropstonepress.com
Purchase this book and others at http://www.creekstewart.com

Published by DROPSToNE PRESS
ISBN 978-0-9976906-9-9

dropstonepress.com

Disclaimer: By using/reading this book, or making a purchase, user agrees as follows:

The information, services and products are sold or given to the user with the understanding that neither the author, seller, nor publisher is engaged in rendering any legal, business or financial advice to the purchaser or to the general public. Although we make strong efforts to make sure our information is accurate, Creek Stewart & DROPSToNE Press cannot guarantee that all the information in this website and or blog is always correct, complete, or up to date. By purchasing any of our products or services, user agrees to and is knowingly assuming any and all risk associated with using these products or services.

TO THE MAXIMUM EXTENT PERMITTED BY LAW, THE PRODUCTS, SERVICES AND INFORMATION IN THIS BOOK IS PROVIDED "AS IS" AND WITH ALL FAULTS AND Creek Stewart & DROPSToNE Press MAKES NO PROMISES, REPRESENTATIONS, OR WARRANTIES, EITHER EXPRESS, IMPLIED, STATUTORY, OR OTHERWISE, WITH RESPECT TO THE PRODUCTS, SERVICES AND INFORMATION, INCLUDING ITS CONDITION, ITS CONFORMITY TO ANY REPRESENTATION OR DESCRIPTION, OR THE EXISTENCE OF ANY LATENT OR PATENT DEFECTS, AND Creek Stewart & DROPSToNE Press SPECIFICALLY DISCLAIMS ALL IMPLIED (IF ANY) WARRANTIES OF TITLE, MERCHANTABILITY, NONINFRINGEMENT, FITNESS FOR A PARTICULAR PURPOSE, LACK OF VIRUSES, ACCURACY OR COMPLETENESS, QUIET ENJOYMENT, AND QUIET POSSESSION. THE ENTIRE RISK ARISING OUT OF USE OR PERFORMANCE OF THE PRODUCTS, SERVICES AND INFORMATION LIES WITH USER.

TO THE MAXIMUM EXTENT PERMITTED BY LAW, IN NO EVENT SHALL Creek Stewart & DROPSToNE Press OR ITS SUPPLIERS BE LIABLE FOR CONSEQUENTIAL, INCIDENTAL, SPECIAL, INDIRECT, OR EXEMPLARY DAMAGES WHATSOEVER ARISING OUT OF OR IN ANY WAY RELATING TO THIS AGREEMENT OR USER'S USE OF OR INABILITY TO USE THE PRODUCTS, SERVICES AND INFORMATION, OR THE PROVISION OR FAILURE TO PROVIDE SUPPORT SERVICES, INCLUDING, BUT NOT LIMITED TO, LOST PROFITS, LOSS OF CONFIDENTIAL OR OTHER INFORMATION, BUSINESS INTERRUPTION, PERSONAL INJURY, LOSS OF PRIVACY, FAILURE TO MEET ANY DUTY (INCLUDING OF GOOD FAITH OR REASONABLE CARE), NEGLIGENCE, COSTS OF PROCUREMENT OF SUBSTITUTE GOODS OR SERVICES, OR ANY OTHER CLAIM FOR PECUNIARY OR OTHER LOSS WHATSOEVER, OR FOR ANY CLAIM OR DEMAND AGAINST USER BY ANY OTHER PARTY, EVEN IF Creek Stewart & DROPSToNE Press HAS BEEN ADVISED OF THE POSSIBILITY OF SUCH DAMAGES. THESE LIMITATIONS SHALL APPLY NOTWITHSTANDING ANY FAILURE OF ESSENTIAL PURPOSE OF ANY LIMITED REMEDY.

NOTWITHSTANDING ANY DAMAGES USER MAY INCUR FOR ANY REASON WHATSOEVER (INCLUDING, WITHOUT LIMITATION, ALL DAMAGES REFERENCED ABOVE AND ALL DIRECT OR GENERAL DAMAGES), THE ENTIRE LIABILITY OF Creek Stewart & DROPSToNE Press AND ANY OF ITS SUPPLIERS UNDER ANY PROVISION OF THIS AGREEMENT AND YOUR EXCLUSIVE REMEDY FOR ALL OF THE FOREGOING SHALL BE LIMITED TO THE GREATER OF THE AMOUNT ACTUALLY PAID FOR THE PRODUCTS, SERVICES AND INFORMATION OR U.S. $1. THE FOREGOING LIMITATIONS, EXCLUSIONS, AND DISCLAIMERS SHALL APPLY TO THE MAXIMUM EXTENT PERMITTED BY APPLICABLE LAW, EVEN IF ANY REMEDY FAILS ITS ESSENTIAL PURPOSE.

Earnings Disclaimer: We have made every effort to accurately represent our products and services. The representation of the potential of our products and services is subject to our interpretation. While the earning potential for people who use our products and services is usually very encouraging, you acknowledge that your earning potential is subject to many independent factors all of which vary from individual to individual and are often out of any individual's control. We give no warranty or guarantee of any kind that you will experience any specific level of earnings by using our products and services. Any examples we have provided should not be interpreted as any guarantee of earnings. We do not assert that our products and services represent a "get rich scheme". Upon request we may assist you in the verification of claims of actual earnings and/or examples of actual results achieved, though we are under no obligation to do so. We cannot and will not offer any direct financial advice, nor are we responsible for any financial decisions that you make. It is your sole responsibility to discuss the legality or financial soundness of any decision you make with a qualified professional before making such decision. Information found in our products and services may contain information that includes forward-looking statements as defined by the private securities litigation reform act of 1995. We base any forward-looking statements solely upon our expectations of events that have not yet occurred. You can easily identify such statements, as they do not relate specifically to any historical nor current facts. These statements use words such as *anticipate, believe, estimate, expect, intend, plan, project*, and other words that imply similar meaning in connection with a description of potential earnings and financial performance. Any and all forward-looking statements used with our products and services are solely based on our opinion of earning potential. As there are many factors that will determine your actual results, we make no guarantees that you will achieve similar or any results from your use of our products and services.

DO THIS RIGHT NOW—
MAKE SURE YOU ARE
ON THE EMAIL LIST THAT
I'VE CREATED FOR SENDING
OUT SUPPLEMENTAL
INFORMATION ABOUT
THIS BOOK.

GO TO
SURVIVALCEO.COM/LIST
TO ADD YOURSELF.

ABOUT THE AUTHOR

Hi, I'm Creek Stewart—I'm a former pharmacy student turned Wilderness Survival Instructor, author, and television host. I'm also a diligent entrepreneur who has figured out, through years of trial and error, how to convert my passion for teaching wilderness survival skills into a very rewarding and fulfilling career.

I'm convinced that we live in a day and age where anyone with a passion and a solid work ethic can build a business around doing what they love and never "work" another day in his or her life!

But it WILL NOT happen by chance.

In this book, I'll tell you exactly how I turned my obscure passion for wilderness survival into a small empire using a proven and repeatable system that I call THE SURVIVAL CEO 5-PILLAR BLUEPRINT.

I believe you can use the same system to turn your own passion for the outdoors into a successful business as well.

Remember, it's not IF but WHEN,

PREFACE

What if you could turn your favorite outdoor hobby or passion into a career? What would it feel like if "going to work" meant that you got to spend time outside doing exactly what it is you love—and get paid for it? Would your life be any different than it is right now?

It's totally possible, and it's not exclusively reserved for those who "get lucky!" In fact, luck has nothing to do with it. If you want to do this, you must stop treating your would-be business like a HOBBY and start treating it like a REAL BUSINESS. Real businesses are built with SYSTEMS, not luck. It took me over 10 years to figure this one out. Passion wasn't enough. I needed a system.

Ultimately, this book is about you. I wrote it because I truly believe that the SURVIVAL CEO 5-PILLAR BLUEPRINT I developed for growing my wilderness survival business can be replicated, by anyone, to build a REAL business around any passion or area of expertise.

Though my focus is entirely centered on helping you, the first couple of chapters in this book are about me. Some backstory on my life will help with perspective and show you how all of this started—and that I'm not anyone special.

Even though thousands of people follow what I do, I can't assume you do. This book could very well be the first time you have ever heard my name. Thus, I feel it's important to give you some context about who I am and where I came from. So, bear with me as I tell you some stories and give you the background on how I reached the point in my life where I understood that I could and should share what I have learned in business with other entrepreneurial-minded outdoor enthusiasts like yourself.

PREFACE

No matter where you're at in your journey—whether you just have an idea or you're trying to take your existing business to the next level—I promise there are valuable nuggets of field-tested gold in this book for you.
I PROMISE.

One thing is certain. If you have a passion for something, the stars have aligned with online technology (and what I reveal in this book) for you to build a profitable, rewarding, and fulfilling business around that passion if you so desire.

I'm excited for you!

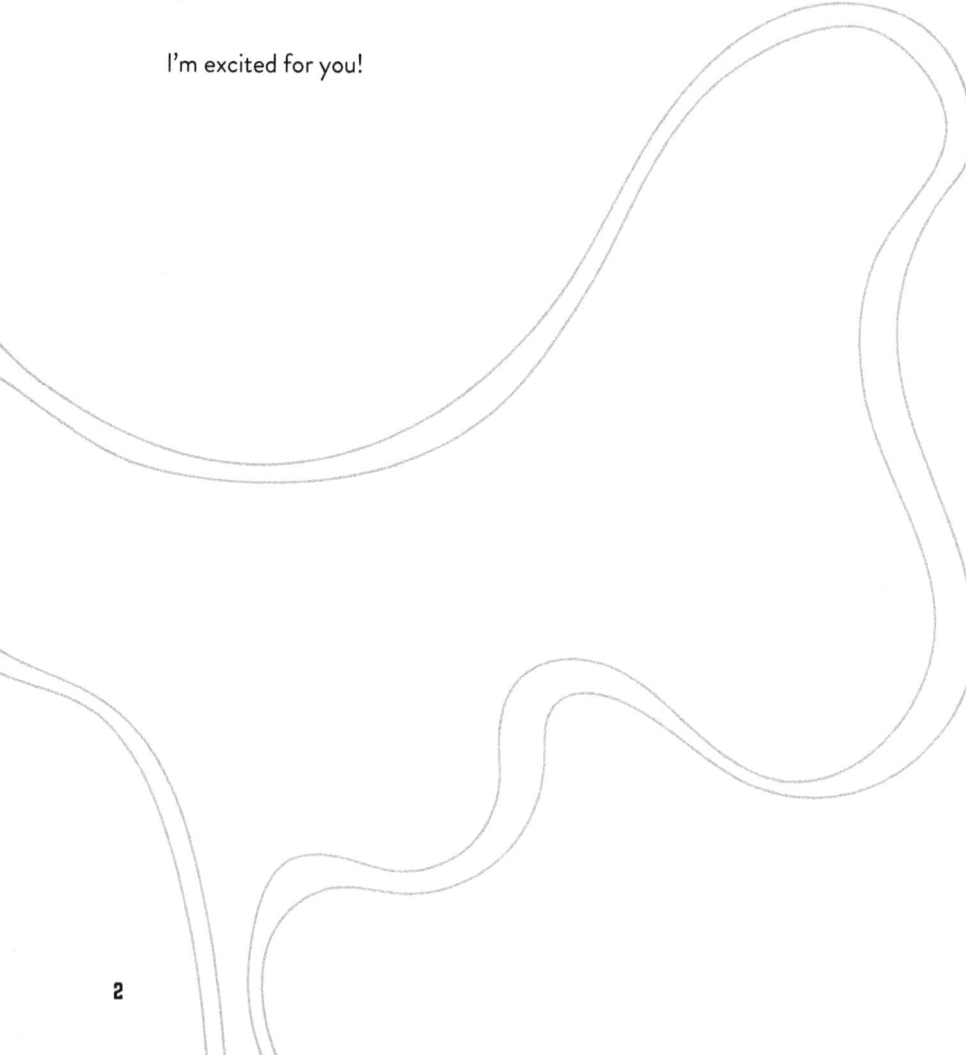

INTRODUCTION: THE SEED

My brother and I got off the school bus and were walking up our driveway on a random Tuesday afternoon. I was about ten years old, and my brother was around eight. For us, that day was just like any other. But for Mom and Dad, it was far from normal.

Earlier that afternoon, my Mom had left work early to run a special errand to the post office, which was very rare. She was a Guidance Counselor for a local high school at the time. On her way to the post office, she noticed that a car was pulled off to the side of the road. As she got closer, she realized it was my Dad's car. But Dad was supposed to be at work. Naturally, she slowed down and edged up behind his car on the shoulder of the road. She got out of her car and walked up to his. As she approached the driver's side window, she saw that my Dad was in the car crying.

Unless it was raining, my brother and I had the same routine every day after school—we'd get off the bus, unlock the door using the hide-a-key, throw our backpacks in the hallway, and run through the yard into the woods to play until Mom rung the huge cast iron dinner bell that was mounted to a post in our yard.

On this day, both Mom and Dad's cars were in the driveway, which was odd. Rather than run into the woods, we excitedly walked inside. They were sitting at the kitchen table. Our excitement was stifled by a somber mood that even the unsharpened sixth senses of two young boys could detect.

After my Dad served in the Army, he and his twin brother went to work at the same factory in Cincinnati (where his parents had worked until they retired). At 5:30 every morning, my Dad, his brother, and his brother's wife would load into the car and make the hour-long commute to and from work. They did this, day-in-and-day-out, for 30 years. Suddenly, that routine

INTRODUCTION

came to a halt.

On that random Tuesday, my Dad, who had worked extremely hard for the same company for 30 years, had been handed a pink slip.

In his late 50s and with no formal education, this was a big deal for my Dad. And, it was a big deal for our family. Working in the factory was all my Dad knew, and he had made good money there. My Mom went back to school in the evenings so she could get into administration at the high school. My Dad took another factory job that he hated, making a third of the pay he was accustomed to, and life went on.

Neither of my parents are or were entrepreneurs. In fact, they're anything but entrepreneurs, although, they did take a stab at AMWAY and raising Chinchillas after my Dad was laid off. Neither of those ventures gained any traction. We did farm, but it was more of a hobby than a business. We only had one entrepreneur in our family—my Mom's brother. He owned a couple of sawmills in Kentucky. I didn't come from a family wired for entrepreneurship.

There is a silver lining to my Dad's story. Well, there are many, but the one that most pertains to this book is that the whole experience planted a seed of entrepreneurship in me that would forever change my life in ways I could have never understood or imagined as a young kid.

MY FIRST VENTURE

Everything happens for a reason. I truly believe that, and this story is a great example. When I was in high school, I had my first product idea. I called it "Monkey Knuckles." I cut some thick grapevine from the woods, bent it into a "U" shape, drilled two holes in each end, and mounted a dowel rod between each end that had three big wooden balls on it. It was essentially a hand-sized back massager made from grapevine and three wooden balls. The user held the grapevine handle and rolled the line of balls on someone's back. It took me an entire day, but I made seven of them. If only Amazon had been a thing then, I'd be retired by now!

A set of my Monkey Knuckles. I keep these on my desk as a reminder of where I started.

I asked my parents if I could go to the big city (Cincinnati) and try to sell them to a store. I'm sure they thought I was insane, but they agreed to let me take the car and go.

I drove to the one place where I knew there were lots of stores—the largest mall in Cincinnati—Tri-County Mall. I was so naive at the time; I had no idea there was a difference between large chain stores and small, independently owned stores. So, I went to the mall and walked into stores like Hallmark, Bath & Body Works, and Claire's Boutique, trying to sell them my Monkey Knuckles. All of them, of course, said I had to contact someone at their main office. After being rejected by just about every store in the mall, including Sears, I decided to head back home.

On my way out of the mall, I noticed a tiny store tucked into a hallway. It sold gift-type stuff, and I decided to give my sales pitch one last shot. I didn't know it at the time, but it was an independent store, owned by a local entrepreneur, who also happened to be working the register that day.

INTRODUCTION

I walked in and gave my pitch. The older lady was much nicer (and more receptive) than the managers at the chain stores. She listened to me and even asked a couple of questions about my product. I felt like a real salesman.

After I was finished, she reached under the counter and pulled out a small basket. "Here," she said, "put them in here and I'll display them next to the register."

"You're buying them?" I asked her, almost in disbelief.

"On consignment," she replied.

"What does that mean?" I asked.

"It means you get paid when I sell them," she answered.

She then spent a couple of minutes giving me one of my first business lessons about how consignment works. I soaked it up like a sponge—one entrepreneur learning from the experiences of another.

I couldn't wait to get home and tell my parents! When I did, I think my Mom was as shocked as I was. I could tell she really admired the fact that I set out to the "big city" and got those Monkey Knuckles displayed for sale in an actual store.

A week later, the store owner called and told me she had sold them all and asked me to come pick up my check. I couldn't believe it!

Why am I telling you this? Well, this story is partly why I decided to write this book. It's my version of paying it forward. That shop owner took the time to invest in me, and it made a difference in my life. This book is my way of helping other entrepreneurs who have a passion for the outdoors. If

INTRODUCTION

you're reading this, then you probably either are or want to be an entrepreneur, and you'd prefer to pursue your outdoor passion for a living—or at least part-time. I mean, who doesn't?

I've learned my fair share of business lessons in the 25 years since hocking my Monkey Knuckles at the mall, and all those lessons created the pathway for me to finally do what I LOVE for a living—teach wilderness survival skills and spend more time outside in the woods.

In this book, I'm going share the strategies I used to really drive the success of my wilderness survival training business. I started this business from absolutely nothing, with almost no money, and grew it into a 7-figure business that has allowed me to forge a wonderful life doing what I LOVE. It's rare that a day goes by when what I do feels like work. I spend a lot of time in my favorite place—the woods. The icing on the cake is that I get to teach people skills that could save their lives one day. I get to do good in the world and leave a legacy for my family. I'm guessing you'd also like to make a difference in the world by sharing whatever it is you love to do, right? I'm also guessing that you'd like to spend more time outside. I get it.

Trust me when I tell you that there are few things in the world more fulfilling than waking up and doing what you love every day, especially if that also involves helping people.

As we move forward, don't get hung up on the wilderness survival aspect of my business. If you're wanting to start a wilderness survival business of your own, then this book can be your EXACT roadmap. However, I am 100% convinced that in today's digital age, anyone can build a brand and business around what they love—I don't care what it is. I believe that what I am about to share with you applies to almost ANY business imaginable, especially if you are a solo-preneur who is hoping to build a business based on your own unique skillset, expertise, gifts, or talents. It doesn't matter if you're a rock climber, archer, wood carver, yoga instructor, runner, hiker,

INTRODUCTION

passionate camper, blacksmith, arborist, gardener, fisherman, urban farmer, beekeeper, florist, or wild plant enthusiast—if you are a person who wants to start or grow a part-time or full-time business around doing what you enjoy, then there is something in this book that will help you do it—I guarantee it.

Oh, remember those Monkey Knuckles I sold on consignment at that small, independent shop in the mall? Several years later, while digging through boxes in the basement of my parents' home looking for Christmas decorations, I found them all in a shoebox that had been tucked away at the back of a shelf. My Mom had snuck away to the mall and purchased all my Monkey Knuckles. That's the kind of Mom I have—the best.

But our Moms can't keep us in business forever, can they? At some point, we must build a REAL business that is sustainable all on its own. I would spend the next 15 years of my life figuring all of this out the hard way. I wish I'd had this book back then!

Creek as a young scout with his mom and dad.

CHAPTER 1:
THE STRUGGLE WAS REAL
(THE LAST CHAPTER ABOUT ME, I PROMISE)

It is immensely important for you to understand that my level of success in the wilderness survival training business was not handed to me, and it did not happen overnight. No one in my family was a Wilderness Survival Instructor. No one in my family was even an entrepreneur! In fact, my parents wanted me to be a pharmacist. I grew up in a small town, and our local pharmacist seemed to have it all together. He had a nice house, a nice car, and seemed to really enjoy helping people. I guess for my parents (and for me, to a certain degree) being a pharmacist seemed like a great idea for a stable financial future. One of the best pharmacy schools around was Butler University in Indianapolis, so that's where I went.

I grew up on a farm in Southern Indiana. My idea of a good time was a bonfire and camping in the backwoods with my buddies. I didn't go to the city much. I think I'd been to Indianapolis a whopping 3 times before I moved there for college. I much preferred the country.

I'm a very private person and tend to be a loner, so I opted out of the whole fraternity/Greek life scene. Before long, I knew every patch of woods and nature area on campus by heart. The first year and a half of classes were all general education, so being a pharmacy major still felt like a good career path, as far as I could tell.

However, I spent most of my free time fueling my growing interest in entrepreneurship by dabbling in a few small money-making ventures. One of my most lucrative was operating as the dormitory barber.

CHAPTER 1

By the middle of my freshman year, I was cutting the hair of most of the guys in my dorm. The campus barber was ridiculously overpriced, and his schedule was horrible. For $5, I'd give a decent haircut in the bathroom down the hall (I FOUND A NEED AND SOLVED A PROBLEM). I even hired my neighbor to manage the appointments. He knew my class schedule and I paid him 10% to take the calls and fill my bookings.

Before long, word spread throughout campus, and apparently it even reached the campus barber because I got a call from university administration explaining that I wasn't allowed to run a business in the dorm, and my business was affecting the barber's business. So, rather than charge for haircuts, I switched to "donation only." It's not a formal business if you don't charge people, right? Ironically, on average, people donated more than $5 for a haircut, so my profits INCREASED. Take that you free-enterprise-hating communists!

Long story short, that business would teach me one of the most important business lessons of my entire life. To get customers, I posted flyers on the inside door of all the men's bathroom stalls that read "FREE HAIRCUT in your dorm—CALL XXX-XXXX." That's right, all first-time cuts were FREE. That's how I hooked them. It was a no risk deal for them (financially at least), but for them to come back, I had to do a good job and deliver value. So, with every first cut, I focused on FOUR things:

1. Giving them a good haircut
2. Establishing a relationship
3. Booking the next appointment
4. Getting their phone number so that I could call them with a reminder

An almost identical model would end up being a MAJOR key to how I

CHAPTER 1

would eventually make huge strides in my wilderness survival business, almost 20 years later. We'll get to that soon. For now, I want to generalize those FOUR things into the basic business lessons below, which would ultimately become foundational pillars for my current businesses(es):

1. Give them something of VALUE for FREE
2. Get their contact information
3. Build a relationship with your customer
4. Try to get them to come back for more (and hopefully buy something)

Be sure to remember these things, because we're going to be touching on them throughout this book. In fact, these four steps are the backbone of my current business.

My real wake-up call came my sophomore year of school, when I shadowed a pharmacist. No offense to my pharmaceutical friends, but I asked to go to the bathroom, hung my white pharmacist's jacket on the paper towel dispenser, and ran for the hills.

I had a real dilemma. I knew I didn't want to be a pharmacist. Unfortunately, I didn't have any ideas regarding what I'd like to do instead, until the crow incident.

Yes, a crow. You know, the bird—black with an annoying call. Well, there was a certain crow that came every morning to the yard just outside my dorm window. It always came early and made an insane amount of noise, squawking and calling. Its call echoed throughout the small grass courtyard and tormented me each morning while I was trying to sleep. Somehow, this daily diatribe of squawks and cackles summoned my inner woodsman that the city and college life had so subtly repressed. I decided to set a snare for that crow, which I had named after one of my least favorite pharmacy professors.

CHAPTER 1

Creek getting ready to battle the crow.

I still remember the thrill and challenge of building that snare. I was trying to outwit one of the most intelligent and alert birds on the planet. As time has passed, a lot of the memories from my college years have faded, but I remember that crow incident like it was yesterday. Everything had to be perfect—the trigger I carved from the pine tree in the parking lot, the knots I tied into the dental floss line, the bait, the placement, the timing—everything! It was me against the crow's pure instinct. It was bird-animal against human-animal. In that moment, I was a primitive hunter in the small courtyard of my college dormitory. Then, it happened. I caught the crow!

Don't worry, I didn't have the heart to kill it, so I let the crow go. It never once came back after that. I still thank the good Lord every time I see a crow because it represents a time when something changed in me.

CHAPTER 1

THE MOMENT OF ACTION

If you ever want your dreams to come true, then you must STOP THINKING and ACT! Soon after the crow incident, I decided to take steps toward what I determined was my long-term career goal: TEACHING WILDERNESS SURVIVAL SKILLS. I switched to a business degree and started building my wilderness survival business immediately.

MY FIRST BOOK

I spent most of my free time during my sophomore year at college writing my first survival manual. It was a 90-page, self-published book with hand-drawn sketches of the survival skills I knew at the time—which wasn't much. I didn't make excuses. I moved forward. No, I wasn't qualified to write a survival book. In fact, I wasn't qualified to write any kind of a book on any subject. No, I didn't have a publishing contract. I also didn't have any money. However, I didn't let any of that stop me. I pushed forward anyway and made no excuses that might somehow allow me to quit. When my friends were down the street partying, I was writing, drawing, and researching. Oftentimes, in order to be successful, you must do what others aren't willing to do. You must be willing to make sacrifices. That was just fine with me.

I photocopied my book at Kinkos and had them spiral bound. In my mind, I was a published author! Nothing could stop me!

OFTENTIMES, IN ORDER TO BE SUCCESSFUL, YOU MUST DO WHAT OTHERS AREN'T WILLING TO DO.

YOU MUST BE WILLING TO MAKE SACRIFICES.

CHAPTER 1

I remember sitting at my desk staring at a big pile of homemade survival books thinking, "OK, now how am I going to sell these?" I learned that it is much harder to sell a book than to write one. Later that year, I taught my first Wilderness Survival Course on my parent's farm in Southern Indiana. About 15 people showed up, including a local newspaper reporter. Below is a picture she took of me teaching some Boy Scouts how to flip people off. Okay, I'm really teaching them how to whistle loudly for signaling, but that picture still cracks me up!

Creek's first survival training publicity photo in a local newspaper.

CHAPTER 1

KEEPING THE EMBER ALIVE

That was essentially the beginning of me teaching wilderness survival skills. I'd soon find out that it was going to be very difficult for me to make a living at it (at least using that model). I think you know you're on the right path when your passion for your business doesn't die, even though you aren't getting the positive feedback you want. Even though I couldn't make a living with survival skills and writing at the time, I still LOVED doing it. I believed (and still do) that the skills were important, and I enjoyed (and still do) working with people. I wanted to teach survival skills as my career, but I had to make money and pay bills too. For many years, teaching courses and selling books was supplemental income, oftentimes negative income. If I taught survival skills for the money, I would have quit in my first year for sure. I could not have survived, financially, for very long if I hadn't been working other full-time and part-time jobs.

Creek posing with his first book.

CHAPTER 1

SUCCESSFUL PEOPLE MAKE A HABIT OF DOING THE THINGS THAT UNSUCCESSFUL PEOPLE DON'T LIKE TO DO.

— Herbert Grey

CHAPTER 1

Over the years, I learned what things worked and moved my business forward. I began to discover ways of marketing that turned a profit and perfected these strategies as best I could. I slowly integrated them with developing online technologies to build a system that not only made my business profitable, but it helped to even out my cyclical income into a steady stream of business that allowed me to quit all of my other side hustles and focus on what I loved! After 10 years, I finally developed a repeatable and manageable system for turning my passion for wilderness survival skills into a thriving and growing business.

I'm guessing you can relate to some of what I've just described regarding the struggle to get my "hobby business" off the ground.

BACK TO YOU

Now that you know a little background about me and my business, I'm going to share with you some business insights that, quite frankly, some people would charge thousands of dollars for. In fact, I'm certain I will be labeled foolish by some for practically giving it away. The information on the following pages is the exact road map for how I built my wilderness survival training business up to the time of this writing. If I can use this information to build an incredible business and lifestyle around WILDERNESS SURVIVAL, of all things, I am 100% certain that you can do it with your outdoor passion as well.

However, I must also issue this disclaimer: I cannot guarantee your results. Why? Because, while I know the following strategies work, I don't know how much you are willing to work. Your work ethic is the critical component to the overall equation.

I want to briefly discuss timelines. If this book had been available for me to read 20 years ago (and the technology was available to support it like it is today), I could have shaved YEARS and THOUSANDS of dollars off my learning curve. I could have hit the ground running immediately. The strategies in this book, which took me years to figure out for myself (and that only became available with certain recent technological advancements), can now generate someone else results in months, or even weeks, under the right circumstances.

Everything is in place, and what you're reading right now is the playbook. YOUR ACTION is the only missing ingredient.

Without further delay, let's dig in!

CHAPTER 2:
BECOME YOUR BRAND

Oftentimes, solo-preneurs are the face of their brand. If your business revolves around YOUR expertise, then this is almost always true, and what I have to say in this chapter is something you should consider. If your business revolves around YOUR expertise, that means that YOU are YOUR BRAND, whether you like it or not. Customers will likely associate YOU with your brand before your logo, your color scheme, or any of your other marketing or advertising materials.

When a customer interacts with a solo-preneur, they have expectations. From looks to behavior and everything in-between, you DO NOT want to disappoint them.

Let me give you an example. Let's say you follow the blog of a guy who writes articles about how to get better abs. His articles are very good, and his advice seems solid. After following for a few months, he announces there will be a live "ab-defining" workshop in your hometown. You pay the fee and are excited to meet your ab mentor in person. But, when you arrive, the guy you've been following is a little overweight and is wearing a suit.

What's the problem with this? Well, your mentor doesn't have abs, and you wanted him to look the part of guy who teaches fitness, right? Whether anyone likes it or not, this impression affects the overall brand and product of the guy who wants to teach others about how to get better abs. You probably won't remain a customer.

Let's walk through a couple of examples of people who did a great job at "becoming their brand" when it comes to their overall look and feel.

Steve Irwin the Crocodile Hunter: Steve, may he rest in peace, was a classic example of "becoming the brand." What do you think of when you think of Steve Irwin? I think of that khaki zookeeper's outfit—shorts and a button-up short-sleeved shirt. It was perfect for him, and I don't think I ever saw a video or picture where he wasn't dressed like that. I can also mention his name without also calling him "The Crocodile Hunter," and you'll likely know exactly who I'm talking about.

Hulk Hogan: The Hulkster lives his brand, brother! From the spray-tanned body to the blonde hair, goatee, and classic red and yellow outfits, Hulk Hogan is an icon because of his commitment to "the look." The name HULK doesn't hurt either!

I know, these are extreme examples, but I'm hoping you get my point—personal branding is extremely important! It doesn't mean you have to change your name, wear a superhero outfit every day, or be overly eccentric, but it is something you should think about.

Let's take me and my brand, for example. Below is a photo that was printed in a local newspaper when I wrote my first book back in college. I sent a round of press releases, and the editor of my hometown paper called and wanted to write an article. I traveled to their office and he took the photo nearby. I'm wearing pressed khaki pants, a striped button-up collared shirt, and a pair of sneakers.

CHAPTER 2

If you've followed me for very long, I hope that photo isn't what you think of when you hear the name "Creek Stewart." If I've done my job right over the years, hopefully it's more like the CARICATURE rendition of me below.

A recent caricature rendition of Creek.

These days, my publicity photos look like the following:

CHAPTER 2

I think you'd agree that I currently look more like someone you'd expect to see teaching you wilderness survival skills than I did in that first newspaper photo, right?

My "look" now isn't a contrived persona. It is a genuine outward expression of who I feel like and want to be on the inside. It is me owning my brand.

Several years ago, I was invited to be on The Today Show in New York City for a wilderness survival segment with Kathie Lee Gifford and Hoda Kotb. You can be sure I wore my knee-high elk leather moccasins. Why? Because that's **MY** brand!

Creek on The Today Show.

I wish someone would have given me this advice 20 years ago. You'd be shocked at how important the outward expression of "becoming your brand" is in the eyes of your customer.

CHAPTER 2

    More importantly, however, is the effect that EMBRACING your inner brand has on YOU. Don't confuse this advice with being superficial. It's quite the opposite, really. It's more about OWNING who you are than anything else. Embodying your passion from the inside out takes courage. If your business relates to your passion, then becoming your brand will feel like a natural progression. It will be an outward expression of you taking ownership of your interests and passions. The last thing I'm suggesting is trying to become something you're not. That's not authentic and won't feel or look genuine, anyway. Authenticity and true character are at the core of becoming your brand. What I am challenging you to do is to keep this in mind while developing your business because it could make a difference for you. This is obviously more applicable to some types of brands and businesses, but it plays a role in almost every brand that is based on sharing expertise with others.

CHAPTER 2

WHO IS THE PERSON YOUR FUTURE CUSTOMER HOPES TO DO BUSINESS WITH?

CHAPTER 2

Before we close out this chapter, I'd like to share a quick story that helps to further illustrate my point:

When I first bought my training facility, Willow Haven Outdoor (http://www.willowhavenoutdoor.com), it had been abandoned for many years. The windows had all been knocked out, fixtures were stripped and damaged, it had holes in the roof, and the whole building needed to be renovated. Nature was truly reclaiming the place. Long story short, after working on the property myself for a while, I found that there was a bug problem, so I called a local exterminator. When he pulled up and got out of his lime-green pick-up truck, I had to look twice! I thought he was Bill Murray from Ghostbusters. This guy had on what looked like a flight suit, goggles, and a helmet. He was a CHARACTER!

"James?" (that's who the lady I spoke with over the phone had told me to expect) I asked.

"Yep, but most people call me Splat," he replied while licking a big, green sour-apple lollipop.

I immediately knew I had the right guy for the job. Splat took care of business like a champ. In fact, I recommended him to some friends two years later. I'll never forget Splat, or his name.

Every solo-preneur who has expertise to offer the world can take a lesson from Splat. BECOME YOUR BRAND.

As you think about this chapter and your own personal passions, hobbies, or business, I'd challenge you to think about how you can better become the person with whom your future customer hopes and expects to do business. That's different for everyone in all types of businesses, but it's food for thought.

CHAPTER 3: CHOOSE A "SMITCH NICHE"

When my Grandmother would bake cookies, she'd always say, "You have to add just a 'smitch' of salt," while taking a pinch of salt between her two fingers and tossing it into the cookie batter. I've named this chapter for her. A "smitch" is a small amount of something.

I know this is an odd chapter title but finding my "SMITCH NICHE" changed everything for me.

I'm sure you've heard the phrase "niche market" before. A niche market represents a smaller, more focused group of customers who are all looking for a similar solution or product. My niche market is "survival." Pretty much all my customers have an interest in survival on some level.

Years ago, having a niche market was enough. Today, however, it is not.

Technology and the internet have changed that. Those two forces combined have made niche markets easily accessible by other marketers, and consequently, most of the general niche markets are very saturated and competition is VERY HIGH. To be successful in today's internet-based marketplace, ESPECIALLY IF YOU'RE JUST STARTING OUT, you need a niche within a niche. I simply call this a SMITCH NICHE.

CHAPTER 3

TO BE SUCCESSFUL IN TODAY'S INTERNET-BASED MARKETPLACE, ESPECIALLY IF YOU'RE JUST STARTING OUT, YOU NEED A NICHE WITHIN A NICHE.

CHAPTER 3

When I first started out in the survival business, I was all over the place. I was studying and creating content about everything at the same time—traps, fire, water, shelter, etc. I didn't even know what a niche market was! Quite frankly, I was overwhelmed. If I would have known to hone-in on a Smitch Niche in the early days of my business, it could have greatly helped jump-start my success. It would have also helped me focus my very limited amount of time and resources in the area that would have made the biggest impact and return on investment. I happened upon my Smitch Niche through a very interesting story that I will tell you in Chapter 6, but for now, it's important you understand that just choosing a niche market is no longer sufficient in this day and age, especially when you're starting out. In general, the niches are already saturated, and breaking into them is very difficult (and expensive). You must find (or even create) your Smitch Niche. Let me give you a few examples of what I'm talking about:

- A chiropractor that focuses on the specific needs of soccer players
- A personal trainer who specializes in helping new mothers get back in shape
- A female climbing instructor who teaches other women how to climb
- A plumber who deals primarily with environmentally efficient products and fixtures
- A chef who develops Paleo recipes for toddlers
- A photographer whose area of expertise is pets, specifically cats
- A chef that focuses on cooking food outside over a fire
- A Wilderness Survival Instructor who creates products and services about Bugging Out (this will make a lot of sense later when I elaborate on my own story)
- A dietitian that specializes in recipes for people who suffer from psoriasis (I have psoriasis and follow several of these very specialized individuals)

CHAPTER 3

Serving a Smitch Niche doesn't mean you can't serve anyone else within your general niche market. It just gives you a place to really establish your brand and business. It should also align with your own personal passions or interests.

After more than 10 years of being all over the place, my Smitch Niche within the broad survival industry became "How to Build A Bug Out Bag." I'll share the story of how that came to be later, but once I found that Smitch Niche, I started to gain some traction in the survival industry. I began to focus all my content creation on that singular topic. Because I was hyper-focused on a single topic, it became MUCH easier for the people who were looking for information regarding a Bug Out Bag on the internet to find me. I ended up writing a book about it, and within a couple of years, I was being invited on to national morning shows, like *Fox & Friends* and *The Weather Channel*, to discuss the topic as a respected expert.

Creek on *Fox & Friends* discussing Bug Out Bags.

CHAPTER 3

Creek on *The Weather Channel* discussing disaster preparedness.

The power of focusing your time and energy on a very specific subject or solution for a segment of your niche market cannot be underestimated.

No matter what your outdoor passion is, there are an infinite number of Smitch Niches that you can focus on. And, there's probably already something very specific within your category that you'd rather focus on anyway. Here's the great news: If there is a Smitch Niche that excites you, then there are probably thousands of other people in the world who are interested in that specific topic as well. Back in the old days, these people were impossible to connect with. Today, with advances in technology and the internet, these people are magically accessible. You can find them, and they can find you! Heck, there's probably a Facebook group on the internet right now that is full of people discussing (and asking questions about) your Smitch Niche already. If not, start one!

You may not know your Smitch Niche yet. That is just fine. My advice about creating content in Chapter 5 will help you find your voice and your Smitch Niche. For now, all you need to know is that a general niche will no longer cut it. You MUST create content for a Smitch Niche in order to

CHAPTER 3

attract the attention (and potential business) of that Smitch Niche—keep this in the back of your mind as you read this book! In fact, grab a notepad and jot down Smitch Niche ideas as they come to you while you read. Capture the moments of creativity that this book will inspire within you.

    I've developed a brainstorming worksheet, which you can see on the opposite page and can be downloaded for FREE, to help you start brainstorming potential "Smitch Niches" within your general niche market. Simply fill in the large circle with your main niche, then brainstorm Smitch Niche ideas in the smaller circles. Write down the Smitch Niche ideas that you're most passionate and knowledgeable about in the smaller circle that overlaps with the larger main niche. I highly recommend that these should be your starting Smiche Niches when we begin discussing content development in the coming chapters. Download here and print as many pages as you need: http://www.survivalceo.com/smitchniche.

    A NOTE ABOUT THE SMITCH NICHE DOWNLOAD: *Later, I'll be going over the importance of collecting your future customers' emails. I'll be completely transparent with you: The Smitch Niche download is a vehicle for me to collect your email, if I don't have it already. I am making you an offer for something FREE—a Smitch Niche Brainstorming Worksheet—in exchange for your email. When you give me your email, I will give you the worksheet. It's a fair trade. As I will describe in detail, GETTING A POTENTIAL CUSTOMER'S EMAIL should be your new goal in life. If you choose to download the worksheet, I will enter your email into what's called an "email automation." While there is an entire chapter dedicated to this later, it's simply defined as a chain of emails that I've prepared in advance to send out to you at specific times after you download the worksheet. Even if you're not interested in the worksheet, you should enter your email and download it to see the process I will take you through. I will offer value to you over the course of several emails (further building trust and a relationship), then I will probably make you an offer of some kind later. Some version of this process is the LIFE BLOOD of my wilderness survival business. Don't worry—I'll tell you all about it in this manual!*

SMITCH NICHE WORKSHEET

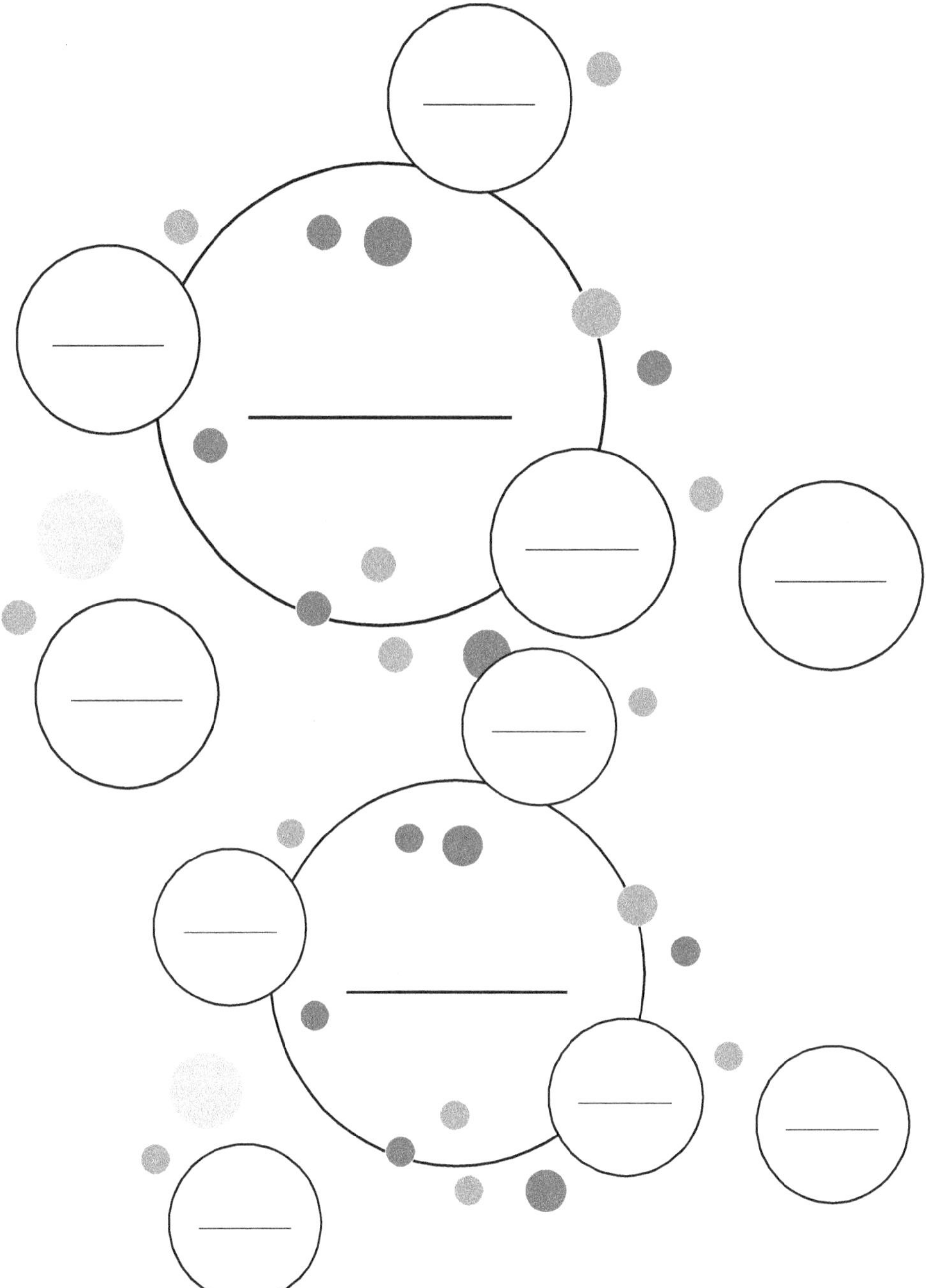

CHAPTER 3

THE 5 FOUNDATIONAL PILLARS

The following several chapters will cover what I call the 5 PILLARS of my SURVIVAL CEO 5-PILLAR BLUEPRINT. These are the FIVE FOUNDATIONAL PIECES I've used (and still use) to methodically grow my business from a daily struggle to an automatic machine that works for me day and night. I am confident that implementing these 5 PILLARS into your business will not only give you focus, but it will give you the traction (and profits) you need to build momentum!

CHAPTER 4: PILLAR # 1: YOUR ONLINE PLATFORM

For you to reach your Smitch Niche and for your Smitch Niche to find and connect with you, you must choose an online PLATFORM to host your CONTENT. CONTENT is what drives traffic on the internet. Don't worry, I'll discuss CONTENT at great length in the next chapter. There are so many content platforms to choose from these days, but the main ones include:

- Blog (writing articles and hosting other various content online; this is the primary platform I use)
- YouTube (or similar online video delivery platforms)
- Podcast (recorded audio sessions)
- Facebook
- Instagram

Building a presence on all these platforms simultaneously is almost impossible and, quite frankly, would be a full-time job in and of itself. It's important (especially in the beginning) to choose just one platform and master it.

When I started, I chose a BLOG as my online platform. If I could do it all over again, I would still make the same decision. A blog has several advantages and specific features for building a real business that other platforms, such as Facebook and INSTAGRAM, do not have. Thus, a blog will be the platform I'll focus on in this chapter. Almost every other platform has limitations that will interfere with the #1 goal—building an email list. The great thing about choosing a blog is that all the other platforms mentioned can feed content and traffic into it, whereas your content is likely limited to a specific platform if you don't go with a blog.

CHAPTER 4

ALL PLATFORMS ARE NOT CREATED EQUAL

As you'll soon discover, your platform's main job is to host valuable content AND provide an online hub for you to gather your potential customer's email. Social media and video hosting platforms, such as Facebook, Instagram, and YouTube, are great for sharing content but horrible for gathering emails. These companies want to keep the subscribers, follows, and likes on THEIR platforms, rather than have you build your own list of "in-house" contacts. These services are great secondary platforms for generating traffic by sharing content but won't directly serve you in your quest for building the life blood of your business—YOUR EMAIL LIST. In my experience, these secondary platforms should be used to drive traffic to your MAIN PLATFORM, where an email can be gathered and used to foster a long-term relationship with your potential customers. Many details about this process to come!

CHAPTER 4

WHAT IS A BLOG?

First, what is a blog? For those who may not be familiar, a blog is a website where you write and post articles about your topic for all to see. Even though blogs are mainly for written articles, you can incorporate pretty much any kind of media into a blog, including social feeds, videos, and even audio tracks. My first blog was http://www.willowhavenoutdoor.com, and it still operates today. In fact, it is still one of my largest organic traffic sources, and I collect countless new leads (emails) from it each day—FOR FREE. At the time of this writing, I've seen over 8,000,000 unique visitors to this blog since its inception. Feel free to check it out to get a better frame of reference as you read this chapter. I own many other websites related to wilderness survival, but my blog is still one of the best vehicles for gathering customer emails. Trust me, if someone enters their email on my blog, they will eventually hear about every other business and service I offer. You'll learn how to do that in PILLAR # 5, which is dedicated to building a relationship (automatically) with potential customers.

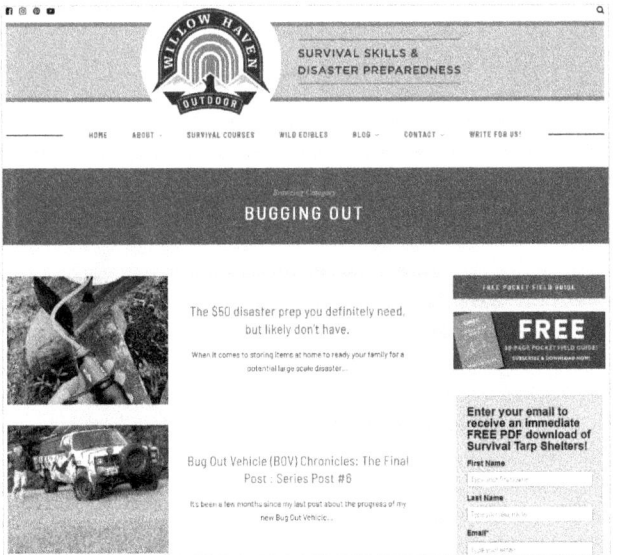

CHAPTER 4

In my opinion, there is no other platform that can allow a single person to develop a legitimate and professional presence almost immediately. Unlike it used to be just a handful of years ago, an online blog allows a boot-strap solo-preneur to create a virtual presence that looks just as good as a Fortune 500 company (or even better)—literally overnight.

The online software platform I use for my willowhavenoutdoor.com blog is one of the most popular blog platforms on the internet—http://www.wordpress.net. According to their website, 31% of the websites on the internet use them (at the time of this writing)! That's a staggering number of sites and speaks volumes for the choice. Besides hosting your website (I host at godaddy.com), it is also completely free (although you'll likely spend some money to get it up and running). I also really like http://www.squarespace.com as a blog hosting platform. It is easy to use and very polished. Their templates make you look like an instant design professional. My website at http://www.creekstewart.com is a Squarespace template site (at the time of this writing). Looks good, right? I built that site in just a couple of hours. Yes, I did it. I didn't have to hire anyone. You can absolutely build your own too! If a Wilderness Survival Instructor can do it, so can you!

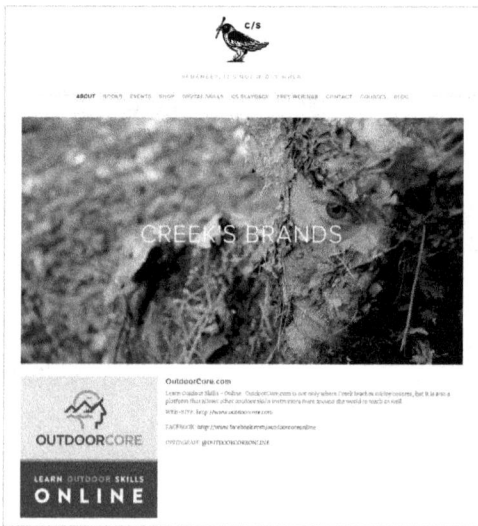

A BLOG IS THE BEST ONE-STOP SOLUTION TO ACCOMPLISH MOST, IF NOT ALL, OF A SOLO-PRENEUER'S PRIMARY OBJECTIVES.

WORDPRESS AND SQUARESPACE COMPARISON

While Wordpress and Squarespace are both blog platforms, they are extremely different. I thought it might be beneficial to give a quick comparison between the two, as I see it. This simple breakdown will save you time researching on your own. Below is a list of PROS & CONS for each platform to help you choose which one you will use to get started.

WORDPRESS:

PROS:

- It's FREE (to start, that is—see CONS).
- You have complete design control.
- There are 100s of PLUGINs to choose from (these are software add-ons that help you achieve a certain task on your blog, for example an INSTAGRAM Plugin to show your INSTAGRAM feed on your blog or an ecommerce plugin so that you can sell products on your blog).
- There are 100s of available templates and themes (while most of these cost money, they can help you get up and running quickly with the design of your site).
- If you can dream it, it can be done in some way, shape, or form on Wordpress.
- Because Wordpress is an opensource software, you have TONS of options when it comes to doing what you want to do. For example, if you wanted to put a contact form on your blog, there are probably 100 different plugins to choose from to do this. Each will look and behave differently. You'll get to choose the one that you like versus being forced to use just one look and feel.

CONS:

- Wordpress does require you to be somewhat internet savvy. If you are not comfortable fiddling around with HTML code, Wordpress might feel a bit overwhelming, and you'll likely have to hire out the design of the site to someone else. Or, you'll spend quite a bit of time "learning" how to use the platform. It isn't difficult, but there is a learning curve.
- While Wordpress is FREE to install, there are some charges to consider. Good plugins and templates are going to cost money. Some are cheap, costing just a few bucks, and others can be a couple hundred dollars. You might as well plan on spending several hundred dollars to get a professional Wordpress site off the ground. This doesn't include designer fees, if you choose to outsource your site's design.
- While anything can be done with a Wordpress site, building one is like putting a bunch of different pieces of a puzzle together from different vendors. All these vendors, including Wordpress, update their plugins, themes, and apps at different times, and it can feel a little disjointed. Keeping everything updated and working as it should requires routine maintenance.
- You must host your Wordpress blog on a separate hosting site like godaddy.com or bluehost.com. Both of those services have a "one-click" Install Option, but whenever you involve more than one online platform, it's just more you have to deal with. Although Wordpress itself is free, you still must pay a monthly hosting fee through wherever you host your Wordpress blog. This can range from $9-$20/month, depending on where you host it.
- You can really screw up a Wordpress blog if you're not careful. Because you'll sometimes need to change code snippets to integrate certain functionalities, there is a possibility that you'll do something wrong, and if you do, it could end in disaster. General rule—don't change any backend code unless you're 100% sure of what you're doing. Always make a backup.

SQUARESPACE:

PROS:

- Squarespace offers many predesigned templates to choose from. Their template themes are amazing and very polished. You choose the template and fill in the blanks or add new ones. You can have a very professional website built in just a few hours. The following websites of mine are all Squarespace templates: creekstewart.com, myapocabox.com, survivalskillofthemonth.com, wildedibleplantofthemonth.com, survivalonthe7th.com, dropstonepress.com, and survivalceo.com.
- No internet savviness necessary. You DO NOT need to know anything about HTML code or the backend of a website to build out a Squarespace blog. The backend is a WYSIWYG (What You See Is What You Get) dashboard, and it is very easy to use with just a little practice.
- Ecommerce is built in. Unlike having to install an ecommerce plugin from a separate vendor like Wordpress, all the ecommerce is prebuilt into the Squarespace platform. Getting approved to accept credit cards takes only a few minutes. Their ecommerce supports both physical and digital products!
- Squarespace is self-hosted, which means everything is hosted right on the Squarespace servers. You can literally do everything, start to finish, right from Squarespace.com and never need to go anywhere else.

CONS:

- Unlike Wordpress, you do not have unlimited creative control over a Squarespace template. You are limited by the look and feel that's prebuilt into the theme.
- Squarespace has a monthly fee. While I feel it is extremely reasonable, basic business plans start out at around $25/month and go up from there.
- Limited connectivity to email software platforms. While you can integrate email collection forms (described in detail later), at the time of this writing I've found limited ability to transfer over information from ecommerce purchases made in Squarespace to my email software. This gives me very limited options for making relevant follow-up and upsell emails based on purchase history at one of my Squarespace sites.

Ultimately, your decision to choose a Wordpress or Squarespace blog will come down to two things:

1. How much creative control do you want?
2. How involved do you want to be in the technical side of your blog?

If you like working with code and the backend-type stuff and want unlimited control and flexibility, then Wordpress is your best choice. If you want an easy blog solution that can meet 95% of your needs and don't like to mess around with the technical side of things, then Squarespace is probably your best choice.

CHAPTER 4

While there are many different online platforms to choose from, a blog is one of the originals. I still believe it is the best one-stop solution to accomplish most, if not all, of a solo-preneur's primary objectives. These include, but are not limited to:

- Posting content about your Smitch Niche (CONTENT CREATION)
- Collecting emails from potential customers and clients
- Selling products, services, or information (physical and digital)
- Booking events
- Hosting online courses (FREE or PAID)
- And so much more!

In PILLAR # 3 (TRAFFIC), I'll focus on the specifics of how I used my first blog (http://www.willowhavenoutdoor.com) as a stepping stone to help propel my brand forward at a much quicker pace than I could have anticipated, including the one secret that changed EVERYTHING for me!

Ultimately, a BLOG is just a framework to host the important stuff—and that stuff is CONTENT. CONTENT is what gets potential customers into your world.

Let me rephrase that: Specific and strategically developed key word rich content that you already know your Smiche Niche is searching for is what gets potential customers into your world.

Remember, success won't happen randomly. It will happen because you have a system in place.

CHAPTER 5: PILLAR # 2: CONTENT CREATION

Even though I've authored over 14 different survival manuals and have written 100s of blog and magazine articles, I didn't start out as a writer. Sure, I wrote my first wilderness survival manual while I was in college, but it was horrible. In fact, I never enjoyed writing in my English classes or even my business classes. But an interesting thing happened when I started to write for my own blog—I liked it. In fact, I grew to love it! Ultimately, I decided that this was for two reasons:

1. I was writing for myself and my future.
2. I was writing about things I liked.

It's amazing what can happen when you begin to write about something you enjoy AND when it feels like you're building something of value for yourself. Makes sense, right?

When most people start out with a business, they chase the money. They pick a business based on what they think will make money. This is ultimately a very unfulfilling decision—whether the money comes or not. This decision MUST be based on what you love to do to have long-term fulfillment. My entire purpose in writing this book is to help you DO EXACTLY WHAT YOU LOVE TO DO for a living.

When I began creating content for my blog, I had no idea what I was doing. I just started randomly writing about topics that interested me. I had no clue about Search Engine Optimization (SEO) or how important it was to write about what people in my market were already searching for. I spent years creating content that would never be searched for and it was a huge waste of time. Now, I create content based upon a checklist of criteria that's founded in SEO analytics and market research. I know that every piece of content I create is going to make me money before I even create it. I could write a book on the topic of CONTENT RESEARCH alone.

JUST CREATE

I'll give you a blog post framework a little later, but right now I want you to understand that CONTENT is important in the world of marketing and promotion. Writing blog posts is one of many ways to create content that can draw in traffic forever. Filming YouTube videos is another way. In fact, YouTube is one of the best ways to market your business in the new online-driven economy. I'll discuss this in detail in the next chapter. When I first started, I committed to writing at least one blog post a week. Developing content fleshes out your platform. An empty platform, whether it be Instagram, YouTube or a blog, is a boring platform. Even if you're able to get people to visit your platform, if there's nothing there, people will leave. And they will likely not subscribe, return, or buy anything.

If you're like me, you're probably wondering what the heck do you write, film, or photograph for a blog post? My answer is to start with topics that SOLVE PROBLEMS. Simply pick a topic within your Smitch Niche that interests you, which SOLVES A PROBLEM, and start filming, writing, or taking photos. JUST CREATE A POST. A good blog post is an equal mix of text and photos. A supplemental video is even better.

FOCUS ON GIVING VALUE

The one thing you need to keep in mind when you're writing blog posts is that you should try to deliver SOMETHING of value to your readers. It doesn't have to be life-changing value. In fact, solving a small problem is a big deal. It can be a tip, trick, something you learned years ago, a personal story that helped you, a reference to an online or offline resource that helped you in your niche—ANYTHING. When it comes to creating content, you should always try to offer SOMETHING OF VALUE, even if it's a tiny something. My goal with blog posts these days is to make people say "I would have paid for that" after reading it.

THE BEST CONTENT TEACHES SOMETHING OR SOLVES PROBLEMS.

CHAPTER 5

A blog is not a journal or diary. I'm going to tell you something that sounds harsh, but it is true: No one who comes to your blog cares about you. They only care about themselves and what your content can do for them. They have only come to your blog because there is potentially something of value to them. They don't want to read boring diary posts about your life (or your kids). They want solutions to their problems. They want to be entertained. They want something that adds value to THEIR LIFE.

YOUR VOICE

As you create content, multiple things will start to happen:

First, you'll find you enjoy covering some things/topics more than others within your niche. You will start to hone-in on your true area of interest within your niche. This may very well be your Smitch Niche! Ironically, this will most likely become the launching pad for your area of expertise later, if you don't already know what that is. Yes, the things that interest you or that you're good at will probably be the core of your business later. Imagine that—building a business about things you ENJOY! What a novel idea! Trust me, they didn't teach me this in college.

You may already know what it is you love and in what direction you want to go. If so, great! This saves some "discovery time" in the beginning.

I think this is a good time to warn you from falling into a very common trap for beginners. Many ambitious entrepreneurs who just start out creating content do what I call "CREATING FOR MONEY." Especially if you hope this project will ultimately become a part-time or full-time job, it's easy to put your own interests and passions on the back-burner and get caught-up in trying to create content ONLY about what you think may bring in money or sales. Trust me, if you write only for the money, your enthusiasm will very quickly fade for this process. In addition to GIVING A SOLUTION that your audience is searching for, your content must intersect with what makes you HAPPY! This is the only way you're going to stick with the laborious process of content creation. If you write for *just the money or just your passion*—ESPECIALLY IN THE BEGINNING—you'll probably fail. Your content must be a healthy combination of solid research and personal passion. Trust me, someone is asking Google about the problems that you can passionately solve right now!

YOU WANT TO ALWAYS BE ASKING YOURSELF THIS QUESTION:

How can something that I like to do or that I'm good at doing add value to someone else's life or solve their problem(s)?

THE ANSWERS TO THIS QUESTION ARE BLOG POST GOLD.

SPEAKING OF GOOGLE

Now that I've brought up Google, I think it's a good time to remind you (once again) that you're creating a "system" here—not a random collection of blog posts. Writing only about what excites you sounds more like a hobby. You want to build a business. The only reason to write a blog post is to attract your perfect customer and (hopefully) get their email.

THE ONLY REASON TO WRITE A BLOG POST IS TO ATTRACT YOUR PERFECT CUSTOMER AND (HOPEFULLY) GET THEIR EMAIL.

CHAPTER 5

This is where the hobby part ends and the systematic business part begins. Your ideal customer is very likely to purchase your product or service. They're in your Smitch Niche. You provide the answers and solutions to the problems or questions they are searching for online. In order to draw in your ideal customer, you must not only write a blog post that solves their problem or answers the questions they're searching for, but you must also write and build the blog post in a very strategic way. It must be Search Engine Optimized so that Google and other search platforms place it right where your customer can see it.

This minor detail is one of a few I'll write about in this book that separates the 99% of "hobby blogs" from the 1% of blogs that are building a real online business for their owners. You want to be in the 1% and I can help you get there.

When I go back and look at some of my early blog posts, they are almost comical! I hardly recognize the writer I was then. My photos were horrible, my content was unoriginal, and I certainly wasn't solving anyone's problems or even teaching them something. I didn't even know that optimizing my blog content for search engines was a thing. I was spending hours every week writing blog posts that would never be found. That was reflected in that fact that there were no comments, no likes, no views, and no shares.

A well-written blog post should serve two completely different audiences. First, you are writing to solve the problem of your ideal customer. Second, you are writing to please Google's search algorithm. If you don't do both at the same time, you might as well never start writing to begin with. But, if you do them both at the same time, something magical will start to happen. You WILL begin to get free traffic. We'll talk a lot about traffic in the next chapter, but it all starts will strategically planning out the content you will create.

CHAPTER 5

ANSWERING THE QUESTIONS YOUR ASKED BY YOUR SMITCH NICHE

We've discussed finding your Smitch Niche. Not only must you figure out who it is you're writing for, but you must also solve their problems and answer their questions. There are several really great online tools you can use to figure this out, but I always start with "Google's Suggested Search." You know when you start typing something into the Google search bar and a list of phrases populate while you're typing? This is Google suggesting search terms and phrases to you based on what OTHER people are searching. If you start by typing in your main Smitch Niche topic, you'll learn a lot about what problems and questions people are asking Google to help them answer and solve. These suggested phrases are based on real search data and can be a good start for choosing a blog post topic that you know people are looking for.

There are definitely more complicated ways of strategically choosing a blog post topic. There are even tools that can tell you how many people are searching that topic each month. This is where things start to become really interesting but are a bit beyond the scope of this book. Regardless, I always start with Google's Suggested Search when choosing a blog topic.

SEARCH ENGINE OPTIMIZING (SEO) YOUR BLOG CONTENT

Once you've determined the main topic (also what I call the "Key Word Phrase") of your blog post, you must write the post in such a way that encourages Google to send it to the top of the search pages when your ideal customer is searching for it. If I would have known to do this when I first started writing my blog, I'd probably be retired right now! It wasn't until I started to understand the importance of writing for Google, as well as my ideal customer, that my blog posts started to really get some online action (and begin to generate revenue).

I've since systemized these SEO tactics into an 8-Point Checklist that I use every time I write a blog post. Making your blog posts Google friendly isn't hard or complicated if you know what you're doing. The 8 main areas that need to be given special attention are:

- **BLOG POST TITLE**
- **BLOG POST META DESCRIPTION**
- **BLOG POST TEXT**
- **BLOG HEADLINES**
- **IMAGE FILE NAMES**
- **BLOG POST URL**
- **BLOG POST TEXT WORD COUNT**
- **INTERNAL & EXTERNAL LINKS**

I realize this may seem a little confusing right now and it's not my goal to give you a drink from a firehose. I list these 8 points not to overwhelm you with information, but to show you that there are ONLY 8 things you need to do to make Google happy. If you do not make Google happy, Google will not make you happy. It's that simple.

If after reading this book you decide you're serious about building a real business by creating blog content that drives traffic and revenue, I'd love to work with you and help you make sure everything is done right.

But Creek, "I DON'T FEEL LIKE AN EXPERT."

No one feels like an expert of any kind in the beginning. Get over it. If you never start creating content because you don't feel like an expert, then you'll never get anywhere. Do you think I felt qualified to write that

CHAPTER 5

wilderness survival book in college? Heck, no! In fact, I am uncomfortable with the title "expert" to this day, and I am considered an expert in my field almost everywhere I go, in major magazines, and on internationally broadcasted television shows. Don't worry, over time your expertise will grow. When I first started out, I only knew what I'd learned in Boy Scouts about wilderness survival. Guess what—that ended up being a lot more than some people! You don't have to know more than everyone—you just need to know more than some people. And trust me, you already fit that criteria within your Smitch Niche. Your job is to create valuable content for people who know less than you.

Download my FREE Blog Post SEO Checklist
at surrvivalceo.com/seochecklist

YOU DON'T HAVE TO KNOW MORE THAN EVERYONE— YOU JUST NEED TO KNOW MORE THAN SOME PEOPLE.

CHAPTER 5

Here are just a few examples of value-driven blog post content ideas. There are so many more!

1. HOW TO DO SOMETHING: A post like this includes a simple step-by-step tutorial about how to do something within your area of expertise. Here's a post on my blog that is a perfect example: https://bit.ly/2t9R6sn. It teaches the reader how to identify different wood species that work well for starting a fire with the Bow Drill. I get tons of hits to this page from people who are searching the internet for "BEST BOW DRILL WOOD." I answer their questions and offer them a free download (in exchange for their email) for some identification guides. For those who download these guides, I will ultimately invite them to take my MASTER THE BOW DRILL online course. I also offer them other products and services related to making a fire with the Bow Drill, including a pre-carved Bow Drill Kit.

2. A PERSONAL STORY WITH A LESSON LEARNED: There's nothing better for connecting with people than telling personal stories. Generalities are a thing of the past. The more personal you can be, the better you'll connect with your true fans. Personal stories about how you learned something also make perfect teaching moments for you to offer something valuable AND connect with your reader on a deeper level. If you write a post like this, remember that even though the story is about you, it should be written with your reader in mind. How does your story teach them something or solve their problem?

3. CHECKLIST: People love lists. A simple checklist can offer quick and easy solutions to a reader. Lists are easy to write and easy for the reader to digest. And, they offer value. Take these for example:

  a. Top 10 Knots Every Beginning Rock Climber Must Know

  b. Top 5 Foods to Pack on the Appilachian Trail

  c. Top 7 Trees for Making a Bow Drill Kit

      d. 4 Biggest Mistakes Most Wood Carvers Make on Their First Project

4. INTERVIEW: The next best thing to being an expert yourself is interviewing one. An interview with an expert on a subject makes outstanding blog content. Interviewing an expert can provide you with 1, 2, and 3 above! How can the person you're interviewing help your ideal customer?

5. CHEAT SHEET: Cheat sheets are kind of like a checklist, but it has more of a CliffsNotes feel. It teaches how to do something in a short, digestible and easy-to-understand batch of instructions. Here are a few examples:

      a. Trout Fishing Cheat Sheet: The Five Trout Facts You Need to Know

      b. Bow Drill Cheat Sheet: 5 Simple Steps to Starting Fire Using the Bow Drill

      c. Raised Bed Gardening Cheat Sheet: 4 Steps to Your First Raised Bed Garden

      d. Mole Trapping Cheat Sheet: A Step-By-Step Guide to Ridding Your Yard of Moles

6. RESOURCE LIST: This is an easy blog post idea that always generates traffic. It's simply a list of links to useful articles or other online resources that your Smitch Niche might find helpful or interesting. One of the best performing blog posts I ever published was a resource list of 25 different wooden pallet projects. I just found several different sites that made cool things from pallets and compiled them into a list. It still gets TONS of traffic. You can even compile a Resource List of your own blog posts if you've written several that relate to the same subject.

CHAPTER 5

BE ORIGINAL

I don't mean that everything you create must be the first time it's ever been viewed in the universe. Don't put this kind of pressure on yourself. After all, there's nothing new under the sun, right? Completely original, never-before-seen content is very rare these days, but there are ways to make old information your own and give it a fresh, new spin. NEVER plagiarize someone else's content or use someone else's photos! I remember a few years ago I hired an intern to help with posting on social media. This was back when I thought that more social media likes translated to more sales (it doesn't). She posted a photo on our Facebook account that wasn't our own. Well, I got an unappreciative email from the owner of the photo asking why we didn't ask permission and credit them for the photo. They were totally justified in asking this. Needless to say, I apologized and gave them their due credit. It's always better (and just plain ethical) to create original content. It may not be "from scratch," but there is always a way to make it your own—especially with personal stories. With permission, though, using someone else's content can be a great way to build content on your own platform. This is a model used by many popular blogs today. I, however, prefer to be the content CREATOR rather than the content BROKER. In the blog business, the term for this is "aggregation".

PHOTOS, PHOTOS, PHOTOS

I want you to imagine yourself reading a blog post about a topic you're interested in, or maybe you're searching for advice or help. Would you rather just read words or would you rather there be engaging photos (or better yet—video) to accompany those words? The latter, of course, right?

I learned early on that good photos meant more views and more shares—ESPECIALLY on social media and PINTEREST (discussed later). PEOPLE LIKE PHOTOS. PEOPLE REALLY LIKE GOOD PHOTOS.

These days, there is no excuse to have bad photos or worse—no photos at all. Back when I first started, fancy cameras were far too expensive. Now, the camera on my iPhone is better than my $700 DSLR. My advice is to get a cell phone with a good camera. The iPhone has the best camera, hands down (in my opinion). You never know when inspiration will strike. With a camera in your pocket, you'll never miss the opportunity to take photos that can be used in a blog post to provide value to someone. I do it all the time with wild edible plants and things I see that relate to wilderness or urban survival. My iPhone is one of my most important content development tools! I even edit many of my videos on my phone.

In my opinion, you should always include plenty of photos with any blog post you write. It makes the post more engaging, interesting, AND valuable to the reader.

I edit most of my photos these days on my iPhone. The three apps I've found to be most useful are TYPORAMA, CANVA, and PHOTO-FOX. Between these three editing apps, I can essentially do anything with a photo, including laying text over an image.

DON'T EVEN THINK ABOUT IT

You're probably already thinking about how to promote your blog so that people can read it and you can start making sales of some kind. STOP! DON'T EVEN THINK ABOUT IT. I remember when I wrote my first blog post. I was ready to promote my blog to the world. I'm going to give you a valuable piece of information in this process of online development and content creation for the purpose of building a business:

YOU ARE NOT READY TO PROMOTE YOUR BLOG IN ANY WAY UNTIL YOU HAVE A VERY INTENTIONAL SYSTEM IN PLACE TO COLLECT A READER'S EMAIL AND TAKE THEM THROUGH AN AUTOMATED INITIATION AND OFFER PROCESS.

90% OF THE BLOGS (AND OTHER PLATFORMS) I VISIT TODAY ARE FILLED WITH MISSED OPPORTUNITIES, AND I KNOW THAT THE OWNERS, WHO ARE TRYING THEIR HARDEST TO BUILD A BUSINESS, ARE SCRATCHING THEIR HEADS TRYING TO FIGURE OUT WHY IT'S NOT WORKING FOR THEM.

CHAPTER 5

Now, I'm getting a little ahead of myself by giving you this advice, but it's important you hear it now: there are several CRITICAL steps you must take on the back end of your blog so you can make this business you want to build work. Remember, this is a BUSINESS, not a HOBBY. We're building a system, not a random collection of blog posts for fun. Businesses have SYSTEMS in place. Don't worry, I detail all of this later. For now, just know there's some serious STRATEGY that goes into a blog. **It's the one tidbit of information that makes the difference between something you're just doing for fun and something you're doing because you want to build a business.** If you're wanting to build any kind of a business, then you should listen to me. I've done it, and I wish I could go back 15 years to give myself this information. I missed out on so many opportunities because I didn't know what I'm about to tell you. 90% of the blogs (and other platforms) I visit today are filled with missed opportunities, and I KNOW that the owners, who are trying their hardest to build a business, are scratching their heads trying to figure out why it's not working for them. Maybe you already have a blog (or YouTube channel) and you're getting some traffic, but you've not been able to convert that traffic into a real, reliable, and consistent revenue stream. If so, this book (and my training) is going to be a game changer for you.

Now that you understand that VALUABLE CONTENT IS KING, let's start talking about strategy.

POSTING WITH PURPOSE

"But Creek, when do I start selling my product???"

There you go again, thinking about the money.

Unless you're an established business, you likely don't even have a product at this stage in the game. You may have some product ideas. You may even have a few products or services. As you start writing blog

CHAPTER 5

posts that answer the questions your target market is searching for, it is likely your products will change, anyway. Before we start thinking about products, we must find our audience and have an email list building strategy in place. Without an audience, products are irrelevant. It used to be that companies would develop a product and then try to sell it. The better strategy is to develop an audience, then sell them something THEY WANT!

Besides, I am going to tell you, at the end of this book, what I believe is the BEST first product offering you can create for your customer—regardless of your area of expertise! And, it's probably NOT what you think. It took me 20 years to figure this one out!

Blogging should become a part of your new routine. The good news is that you'll be writing about a topic that you enjoy. Remember, ALL THOUGHT LEADERS are CONTENT CREATORS. It is a part of your NEW JOB!

Remember the 4 things I learned as my college dormitory barber?

1. Give them something of VALUE for FREE

2. Get their contact information

3. Build a relationship with your customer

4. Try to get them to come back for more (and hopefully buy something)

This is where we start to really to use your blog to do ALL these things for you. You see, I spent years JUST DOING number 1 with my blog. I was giving away FREE content, expecting or asking for nothing in return. **In fact, I WAS TRAINING my audience to only get free stuff from me.** That is the definition of a hobby, not a business. This was reflected in my bank account, as well. I can't tell you how much I wish someone had given me this information when I was just starting out! If you're an established business with a blog or YouTube channel, are you TRAINING your audience to only get FREE CONTENT from you??? If your answer is yes, don't worry—most people do it. My goal, however, is to give you a system that you can use to CHARGE for your expertise and not just give it away for free all the time!

Here's a scary question—If you're already a content creator, WHO is REALLY making money from all of the content that you're creating? Is it YouTube? Is it the product companies that you promote and review? Is it someone else's blog?

BIG MISTAKE

One of the biggest mistakes I see people make when first developing content for a blog or YouTube channel is thinking that just by creating this content, they will somehow magically make money. THIS IS NOT TRUE! You MUST use your content to generate LEADS. Then you must TAKE THAT LEAD BY THE HAND and walk them through a very specific journey within your business. Don't expect that just because someone finds your content that they will automatically scour your website or platform for something to BUY from you. You must help them with this process. You must take your potential customer by the hand and guide them to the sale. Getting someone to see your content is JUST THE BEGINNING of turning that LEAD into a paying CUSTOMER. Hardly anyone gets this! This is why so many people start a business online and get burnt out! The model of constantly creating FREE content without getting paid DOES NOT WORK for the content creator.

CHAPTER 5

A FINAL NOTE ON CONTENT

Developing content serves several purposes.

First, it establishes you as someone who knows something about your topic. If you know more than whoever is reading your content, then you are an expert on this topic to them. This person becomes a potential customer for either more content, a course (live or online) on the topic, a service related to the topic, or physical products related to your area of expertise. If you don't get their email, then you run the very real possibility of losing them forever. THEY WILL NOT REMEMBER YOU ON THEIR OWN. You must use email to communicate with them over time. I will write much more on this later. Getting them to subscribe to your YouTube channel or LIKE you on INSTAGRAM or FACEBOOK is NOT ENOUGH. You must get their email. YOU MUST GET THEIR EMAIL. We're going to dive deep into this requirement very soon.

YOU MUST GET THEIR EMAIL.

CHAPTER 5

Second, content is how you build your customer database. When I first started posting on my blog, I had no social media accounts, no followers, and no email list. After my first few blog posts, I would call my friends and family and ask them to write a comment on my new post, so it looked like people were reading them. When I look back at my early posts, the comments are from my best friend, my brother, my mom, and my uncle. It's hilarious. You can tell they didn't even read the post!

Third, you will use your CONTENT to actively promote your blog, brand, products, and services. We'll discuss this is PILLAR # 3: TRAFFIC.

But before we do, I must be very clear about one thing—you must do your research and be sure that your Smitch Niche is actually searching for the type of content you're creating. Don't just make a guess based upon what you think because you'll risk wasting your time. ONLY GOOD CONTENT GETS ATTENTION. If your content sucks and you're not answering the questions that your target market is looking for, then expect bad results. Good content should, ideally, meet the following criteria:

- Be well thought out
- Be well-written (have a friend or colleague proofread it for you)
- Contain amazing photos (whenever applicable)
- Teach something or solve a problem (the sign of a true expert)
- Be entertaining—do not make content that feels like you're reading a textbook. Think magazine, not textbook.
- Be unique to you—developing completely original content is almost impossible, but any content can be made unique to you.

Remember, YOUR CONTENT IS YOUR PLATFORM. Without content my system doesn't work, unless you're willing to spend a ton of money in advertising. CONTENT IS KING. Just think of the industry leaders in your niche space for a second. I'll bet they are all content creators—am I right? I'll bet they generate great content that draws people into their world. It may be a blog, it may be YouTube, it may be Instagram, but every thought leader does it. Tribe leaders build their tribe on the back of GOOD CONTENT.

TRIBE LEADERS BUILD THEIR TRIBE ON THE BACK OF GOOD CONTENT.

CHAPTER 5

Great effort should go into developing good content. This effort can pay dividends, repeatedly, for your entire life.

MULTIFUNCTIONAL CONTENT

As a survival instructor, I love survival kit items that have more than one use. For example, I can use a bandana for 100s of survival tasks. This makes the investment in a bandana a smart one, because I can use it for so many different things. As you start to think about creating content, I want you to think about using that content in as many ways as possible. This helps to make your investment of time, money, and energy in creating this content a SMARTER investment. Below are some great ideas to consider for using content in different ways to increase the impact you can have in reaching your audience:

- Compile multiple blog posts on a similar topic into a FREE downloadable eBook (called a LEAD MAGNET—discussed later)
- Compile multiple blog posts on a similar topic into a downloadable eBook that you offer for sale to your audience
- Post the images and an excerpt of a blog post on various social media accounts, including Instagram and Facebook—with the purpose of driving traffic from those platforms to your blog AND benefiting from any SHARES that take place
- If you film a YouTube Video, also integrate that YouTube video into a blog post and share it on all social media platforms to extend market reach
- Turn your blog post into a video and upload it to YouTube for cross-marketing on that platform
- Turn your blog posts into articles that other platforms can use (magazines, industry websites, etc.)
- Create images from your content to be posted on Pinterest to drive

traffic back to your blog in hopes of getting emails.

- Host a WEBINAR where you "bring your most popular blog posts to life"
- Use your most popular blog posts as the foundation for recording a Podcast
- Record your blog posts as you read them aloud and upload them to soundcloud.com to share so people can listen to them while they drive

What other ways can you think of to use your blog posts in a MULTIFUNCTIONAL way to increase reach and exposure?

_____

_____

_____

_____

Now that we've discussed PILLAR # 1: YOUR PLATFORM and PILLAR # 2: CONTENT CREATION, it's time to talk about PILLAR # 3: TRAFFIC. Your platform and content don't matter unless you get your ideal customer to see it.

I've already stressed the importance of writing blog posts that are Search Engine Optimized. Doing this will definitely help to generate organic traffic to your platform. Traffic generated from search engines is my # 1 source of customers. It's very important. But, it's also important to know that there are other ways to generate a lot of traffic.

In the next chapter, I'm going to share some of the traffic secrets I've learned over the years that CHANGED MY BUSINESS FOREVER.

CHAPTER 6:
PILLAR # 3: TRAFFIC

TRAFFIC is simply a tech word for online visitors—people who click to view your content for one reason or another. Everybody and their brother in the online business community is trying to figure out how to get more traffic. Some are paying big bucks in the form of paid advertising to get it. Others, like myself, depend more on other (less expensive) traffic strategies that can serve them for life. The BIG difference between my strategies and paying for advertising is that when others stop paying for advertising, the traffic stops. My strategies keep working long after I've put in the work just once.

With my SURVIVAL CEO BUSINESS-BUILDING BLUEPRINT, your CONTENT will play a major role in driving TRAFFIC to your blog.

In general, there are three types of traffic that will come to your blog:

1. **Organic Traffic:** This is traffic from people who are searching in Google (or another search engine) and happen to find a link to your blog and click on it. You didn't pay for this. Search bots constantly roam the internet and log new pages and new content. These pages then become a part of their search database. Organic traffic is the best kind of traffic, but it's becoming increasingly harder to come by. However, by choosing a Smitch Niche you will already be working within a more concentrated and focused area of expertise. Your organic traffic hits will benefit from this. I can teach you some serious strategies for getting more organic traffic (more on that later).

2. **Paid Traffic:** Paid traffic is when you pay for people to click on a link that leads to your blog. I don't often suggest paid traffic if

you're just starting out. This includes things like paid Facebook ads, paid Instagram ads, Google AdWords, and even taking out advertising space on other people's blogs (Eventually, you can even sell advertising space on your own blog, if you want).

3. FREE-BUT-NOT-FREE Traffic: This is the kind of traffic I will be focusing on in this chapter. This is traffic that is FREE but requires time on your end to make it happen (hence the "BUT-NOT-FREE"). FREE-BUT-NOT-FREE traffic is what changed my business forever. If there is one tangible moment when the needle really started to move with my business, it is when I secured my first FREE-BUT-NOT-FREE traffic source.

Organic Traffic is critical to the long-term success of any well-written blog post. I spend a lot of time making sure that my target audience is searching for what I'm going to write about. I also spend a lot of time choosing the Key Word Phrases for my blog posts so that my organic search reach will benefit. But, Organic Traffic can take 3–4 months for your content to get picked up in search engines like Google.

Paid traffic is great, too, but in the beginning, it can be a little overwhelming and expensive. The third option is my favorite when just starting out because it's free—MINUS a little bit of sweat equity—and it typically yields some really great results.

FREE-BUT-NOT-FREE traffic requires two things:

1. Good content (either written or video) that meets the criteria I detailed in PILLAR # 2: CONTENT CREATION

2. Your time

Let's discuss some of my favorite FREE-BUT-NOT-FREE traffic sources.

CHAPTER 6

FREE-BUT-NOT-FREE TRAFFIC SOURCE #1: ONLINE COMMUNITIES & GROUPS

These days, there are Facebook groups, hashtags, reddits, blogs, and forums for any and every topic imaginable. It is likely you already participate in or frequent several of these within your Smitch Niche. These can be outstanding FREE-BUT-NOT-FREE traffic sources. However, here's where that whole 'great content' thing comes into play. You can't just go posting SPAMMY sales copy in these places. Not only is it not cool, you'll likely get banned and people will just associate your username with "that spammy guy or gal who's just trying to sell stuff." The key here is good, value-driven content that IDEALLY solves people's problems or teaches a skill of some kind within your Smitch Niche.

The places I've mentioned can offer incredible insight into what your Smitch Niche WANTS to learn. In fact, I would highly suggest doing your market research inside of these groups and forums before you even start writing. Find out what questions they are asking. See which threads are most popular and have the most interactions. Uncover what challenges they're facing or what problems they're needing solved. You can even ask what topics they'd like for you to write about. WRITE BLOG POSTS ABOUT THOSE THINGS. Your job, as a business owner, is to SOLVE PROBLEMS. People won't come to you because they want to buy your product. They will come to you because they want to buy your solution to their problem. I went to the hardware store to buy a drain snake the other day. The last thing I wanted was a drain snake to clutter up my already messy garage. What I wanted was for my pipes to drain. I bought the solution, which happened to come in the form of a drain snake!

PEOPLE WON'T COME TO YOU BECAUSE THEY WANT TO BUY YOUR PRODUCT.

THEY WILL COME TO YOU BECAUSE THEY WANT TO BUY YOUR SOLUTION TO THEIR PROBLEM.

CHAPTER 6

Let's take this a step further. If I visited a wilderness survival forum and there was a huge discussion about how to start a fire using the bow drill, how awesome would it be for me to post a message that says something like:

"Hey guys, I've practiced using the Bow Drill for a long time. It's not easy, but there are several tips and tricks that can really help. They're too long to type up here, but I've put them all down in one place if you want to read them. I call it the BOW DRILL CHEAT SHEET and the link is here: XXXXXXX"

Notice I'm not selling anything. I'm just simply including a link to an article I wrote that may help with their frustrations. I'm not only helping people by providing them with FREE, valuable information, but I'm very subtly establishing myself as an expert to those who don't know how to make fire with the Bow Drill. Make sense?

On an even simpler level, you can JUST ANSWER QUESTIONS within these groups. For example, I have a closed Facebook Group for students who take my online fire-starting course called THE ART OF FIRE. While I have the best of intentions to answer all the questions asked from my students in that group, I just don't get to all of them. What I've noticed is that other students sometimes answer these questions. These students are showing their expertise on a subject and slowly developing their authority, one answer at a time. You can do the same thing in groups you are involved with. Just answer questions for people. But be sure to have a link to your blog in your profile so they can find out more information about you. Trust me, if you provide someone a valuable answer, they will likely click on your profile, and if you have a good LEAD MAGNET (discussed later), you'll likely be able to capture their email and woo them into your tribe. Better yet, mention your FREE LEAD MAGNET right in your social media profile description!

On a side note, it's also a good idea to be an established member in an online group or forum before posting any kind of link. Being a member of the community for a while goes a long way in establishing trust. This also helps for your link not to appear spammy in any way.

The one critical piece to this equation for your business is that you make every attempt possible to collect EVERY EMAIL ADDRESS YOU CAN from this FREE-BUT-NOT-FREE traffic that clicks over to your blog. We will discuss specific ways to do this in PILLAR #4: BUILDING YOUR EMAIL LIST.

Visiting forums, groups, blogs, reddits, and the like will not only keep you up to date on the pain-points of your Smitch Niche, but it will provide you with an infinite number of blog posts to write as well. All these blog posts will help drive organic and FREE-BUT-NOT-FREE traffic. Some of them can be fleshed out into FREE, downloadable guides that can be traded for emails (discussed later). The good ones can be the basis for an actual book. In fact, it's time for me to tell you about the one marketing tactic that changed my business forever—almost overnight. This is one of the best FREE-BUT-NOT-FREE traffic strategies of all time.

FREE-BUT-NOT-FREE TRAFFIC SOURCE # 2: WRITE FOR A LARGER AUDIENCE THAN YOUR OWN

Let's face it, no matter what you do in the beginning, you're not going to have a very big audience. It will slowly grow as organic traffic starts to build up and as people share your blog posts on social media, but it's a process that takes some time. However, I discovered one trick late in the game that changed the face of my business FOREVER. In fact, I'll say that I wouldn't be where I am today without it!

CHAPTER 6

Several months, maybe even a year or so into writing blog posts, I continued to beat my head against the wall, trying to get more traffic. My email list was slowly growing with organic traffic (even though I hadn't yet figured out how to boost it with strategic SEO prinicples). I had no social media following (in fact I had NO social media accounts at that time). Even my Mom stopped posting comments. I also didn't have any money, so I couldn't PAY for traffic or buy ads. In order to grow at all, I was in desperate need of TRAFFIC—and it had to be FREE.

One day, out of the blue, I received an email from a company that sold ammunition. The lady asked if she could write what she called a "GUEST BLOG POST" about survival gun ammunition. She even asked if there was any specific kind of ammo she could send me to try out. Besides a few random comments to date, this was the first time anyone made me or my blog feel valuable. SHE wanted to write for ME—and give me some ammo—all for FREE. By that time, I was pretty tapped out on writing blog posts and was very open to the idea of someone just handing me one. So, I agreed and a few days later she emailed me a well-written, relevant blog post for my subscribers. She also asked if I could link the different ammunition she discussed in the post to the pages where they sold it on their website. I agreed to do that and had the blog post up in just a few hours. A few days later I received a box of ammo in the mail. It was a pretty cool arrangement.

Let's talk about what just happened.

First, as a blogger, I was and am always in need of content that relates to my audience. I was happy to not have to write a blog post and let someone else do it. Also, I got something in return for it! Second, the ammunition company received exposure from MY AUDIENCE, all of whom had probably never heard of them before. You see, every time I write a blog post, I email everyone on my email list about it. I don't remember how many email subscribers I had at the time, but it was probably a few hundred. I know it's a relatively small number, but that's not the point. THE POINT is that this was a WIN-WIN proposal and SHE gained new exposure for minimal cost. In fact, I would have agreed to do it without the offer for free ammunition, because survival guns and ammunition was a popular topic for my audience anyway.

Well, this little business exchange between the ammunition company and myself got me thinking: What if I tried to write a guest blog post for someone else's blog who has an audience BIGGER than my own? If they agree, I will gain immediate exposure to THEIR subscribers and maybe some of them will become MY subscribers. And just like that, this concept became my new obsession.

Over the next several weeks, I emailed as many different blogs that I could think of and find. I tried to choose blogs that weren't necessarily all about wilderness survival. Those people may see me as a threat or competition, so I selected blogs whose audience might appreciate my type of content. These included blogs in the genres of men's interest, homeschooling, gardening, hiking, and camping. They weren't survival specific, but I imagined that survival would be of interest to them and their audience. I simply introduced myself to the blog owner through their contact section, gave them the link to my blog, and let them know that if they ever wanted a blog post about wilderness survival or disaster preparedness, I'd love to write an ORIGINAL POST with ORIGINAL PHOTOS for them. I even gave a few ideas for sample post topics in the email. I didn't ask for ANYTHING in return. Not yet, at least.

I received a lot of no's, of course, but one day I received a YES from a HUGE men's interest blog. On the next page is the exact email:

CHAPTER 6

Hi Creek-

I was wondering if you might consider doing a post for us on making a bug out bag. I know you plan to do it for your site as part of your series on the four aspects of bugging out, but what you could do is take some of the intro to that main post to start it off and then flesh out just the bug out bag for us. We've had the bug out bag on our future post to-do list forever, so that would be awesome. But if you're not interested, that's okay, too.

I was over the moon. Before I tell you the rest of the story, this is where I preach to you about CONTENT again. You can guarantee that every person who considered my proposal of writing for their blog visited my website and reviewed the kind of content I created. If my content was crappy, do you think they would have even considered my offer? CONTENT IS KING! You must produce original quality content—with AWESOME photos.

Ok, back to the story. I immediately agreed and promised to have the post ready within a few days. I worked my butt off on that post. I did the absolute best I possibly could at the time, and I was nervous to send it. Below is the email I received after I did:

Creek-

Holy smokes. Your post is awesome! Really, really awesome--you simply hit it out of the park. Thanks so much for the work you put into it and for doing this. I'll be publishing it next Monday night.

I WAS SO PUMPED!

Oh, I almost forgot the most important part—the blog owner asked me to provide them with a 1–2 sentence byline. I didn't even know what a byline was and had to Google it. It's just a line or two identifying and crediting the author. At the time, I was willing to write this post with just the mention of my name or my training facility somewhere. A byline was even better! Below are the two options I sent them. You can model your own byline after one of these:

Creek Stewart is a Senior Instructor at the Willow Haven Outdoor School for Survival, Preparedness & Bushcraft. For more information, visit http://www.willowhavenoutdoor.com.

Creek Stewart is a Senior Instructor at the Willow Haven Outdoor School for Survival, Preparedness & Bushcraft. Creek's passion is teaching, sharing and preserving outdoor living and survival skills. For more information, visit http://www.willowhavenoutdoor.com.

I didn't ask for ANYTHING in return. No links. No spammy requests. No affiliate links. I didn't try to sell anything. I didn't do anything weird. Don't be weird! Just focus on trying to provide VALUE to THEIR audience and everything else will take care of itself.

That blog post changed my business forever. When it was published, I immediately received 100s, maybe even 1000s of new followers. They wanted MORE! Remember when I discussed finding your Smitch Niche? For the next several years, BUG OUT BAGS and everything BUG OUT-related became my Smitch Niche.

In fact, this one blog post led to my first book deal. After the blog post was released, I received an email from an Acquisitions Editor at a major publisher asking if I'd be interested in writing a full-length book about how to build a bug out bag. Thus, began my first official book deal for Build the Perfect Bug Out Bag, which is still a best-selling title that has sold thousands of copies. Again, CONTENT is KING!!! That great piece of content I wrote for someone else's blog led to a very successful three-book series about Bugging Out and 1000s of new followers to my blog.

CHAPTER 6

Ultimately, I used my books about bugging out to get featured on countless morning news programs, blogs, news websites, podcasts, and radio shows. I also used them as a platform to teach live courses (paid), host live webinars (lead-generating), book numerous speaking gigs (paid), sell products (paid), and truly establish myself as an authority on the subject (Bugging Out) within my Smitch Niche (priceless).

DO NOT become obsessed with landing a guest post on a major blog with one million subscribers. Just try to find blogs with a larger reach than your own (that's easy in the beginning), which market to readers who may also be interested in your content. I've put a few lines below. I want you to take a few minutes and brainstorm some markets that may have cross-over interest in your Smitch Niche.

_____

_____

_____

CHAPTER 6

Nowadays, every blog has a Facebook page. A good way to get a general sense for the reach of a blog is to see how many Facebook followers they have. Everyone, except for me I think, is obsessed with getting Facebook followers. I am obsessed with getting email followers. Did you know that Facebook only delivers your post a small percentage of the people who like your page? You must pay for it to be delivered to more of the people who LIKE your page. However, every email I send gets to all my customers and stays in their inbox until they delete it. Once someone scrolls past your post on Facebook, you might as well consider it gone forever. You'll soon find out that I believe the most important thing you can do as a solo-preneur, who has advice, expertise, or content to share with the world, is to GET THE EMAILS OF EVERYONE WHO VISITS YOUR BLOG (or any online platform that you operate). Again, I digress. More on this in the next chapter.

Since I started my blog, it has become a huge organic traffic generator for me. It ranks very well within several different wilderness survival topics and is consistently ranked as one of the Top 50 Survival Blogs on the internet. I receive 1000s of organic impressions per month. As my business grew, writing blog posts became less of a priority for me, but all that past hard work continues to drive traffic for me, today! That's another great thing about a blog. It's like a survival trap in the woods, it will continue to work for you around the clock, passively. Build it once and it lives FOREVER!

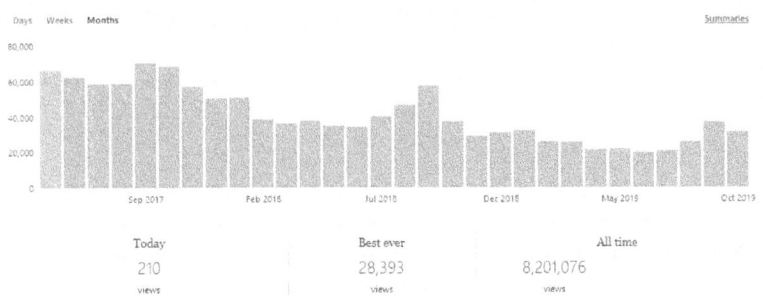

Analytics screen capture (at the time of this writing) from Creek's blog at willowhavenoutdoor.com—over 8,000,000 views since inception.

CHAPTER 6

Each week, I receive at least 3 requests from someone or some entity asking to write an article on my blog. Almost ALL of them are sent via an automated email robot. They aren't personal. They don't mention my name. They never mention a specific blog post, and it's clear that whomever or whatever sent the email has never even visited my blog, revealing that they do not care about my readers. I NEVER, EVER, EVER, EVER respond to these emails. Below is a great example of what I'm talking about. I actually received this email while writing this book. The timing couldn't have been better!

Hi There,

I am writing because I would like to write an article on how to plan your honeymoon. My wedding day was one of the best days of my life. Planning it was highly stressful and because of that we did not put the same level of planning into our honeymoon. That was a mistake. My name is Jane and after spending a decade working in the tourism industry, planning tours, I really should have known better.

From picking a good location to activities, hotels, and so on, it's difficult to get everything right. It means knowing your future spouse and knowing what kind of honeymoon you want, whether it's relaxing, romantic, or adventurous. I'd like to correct my mistakes by writing an article for you on this topic.

While researching a new article, I came across willowhavenoutdoor.com. My focus on honeymoons seemed like a natural fit and I was wondering if you would let me write an article on this topic. All I would ask in return is that any resources and references, including to a tech review site I work with, is included.

Please let me know if we can work together.

Best Regards,

Jane

CHAPTER 6

So, yeah, apparently "Jane" thought attending a survival course would make for a great honeymoon! This is a perfect example of someone requesting to write a guest post on my blog who has NO IDEA about my business or market. Not only is it a topic on the opposite end of the spectrum from SURVIVAL, but it would have NO APPEAL whatsoever to my readers. In fact, they would probably unsubscribe from my email list if I sent them a blog post about how to choose a honeymoon spot. Ridiculous!

So, what's my point? Guest posting has become a very popular way for companies to gain exposure through blog traffic. As much as I'd like to think I'm the smartest blogger on the planet—I'm not the first person to figure out that this is a good method for scaling quickly. The blog that you're wanting to write a guest post for will likely receive other requests. It's important that you stand out. The way you do that is by being personal. NEVER send generic form emails to blogs! DON'T COPY AND PASTE THE SAME EMAIL TO MULTIPLE BLOGS. This is not personal. Write each email individually and make it feel personal. Study their blog. Read some of their posts. Read some of their comments. Follow them on Facebook and Instagram. Get to know the blog and their readers a little bit before asking them if you can write a guest post. Then, when you send them an email, draw on this personal information. Below is a sample email request I sent to a blog years ago. It was a blog that focused on SLINGSHOTS and SLINGSHOT SHOOTING. Not only was I genuinely interested in the subject, but I felt I had real value to share with the readers, so I put together an idea and emailed it off. Here is what I wrote:

Name-

My name is Creek Stewart. I am a Survival Instructor and host a blog, myself, at http://www.willowhavenoutdoor.com.

Your blog is awesome! I found it while researching slingshots so I could write a slingshot-related post for my own blog. I think my favorite article so far

CHAPTER 6

is the one you wrote about how to use a natural tree fork to make a slingshot. It's perfect for my survival-minded readers and I even included a link to it in the last email newsletter that I sent out. I told them to tell you Creek sent them!

I'm in the middle of writing a blog post titled SURVIVAL SLINGSHOTS and it's basically a collection of slingshots made from everyday items that can be used to hunt small game in a survival scenario. It's pretty cool. I've figured out ways to make slingshots from cardboard, PVC pipe, and a U-bolt, and I have ideas for how to make band sets from swim caps and even condoms! I also have awesome pictures of each one! I've attached a couple for you to see.

I'm writing today to see if you would be interested in being the FIRST & ONLY blog to publish this article. I think your readers would really dig it. I even saw a few comments on your post titled HUNTING WITH A SLINGSHOT about using makeshift items to make a survival slingshot.

I'm not asking for anything in return. I'm not selling anything, and I'm not interested in embedding any weird affiliate links (I get those requests all the time). My goal is to provide you with some awesome content in hopes of gaining a little bit of exposure for my own blog with some of your readers who may have an interest in survival as well.

Let me know if you'd be open to a guest blog post!

Thanks for your time.

Creek Stewart

[CONTACT INFO]

The owner of that blog agreed to let me write the post. I was able to garner the interest of countless people who had an interest in SURVIVAL and SLINGSHOTS. This post not only provided value to the blog owner, but it also allowed me to silently find MY tribe within HIS tribe. Unfortunately, that blog eventually went under, but I liked my post for him so much that I (years later) fleshed it out to create one of my best-selling Pocket Field

CHAPTER 6

Guides titled SURVIVAL SLINGSHOTS. I now sell 100s of these each year, and they ship all over the world. Remember, I always look at a blog post as a potential "outline" for some kind of a future guide or manual, either printed or digital (or both), to sell for profit or use as a LEAD MAGNET for a potential customer's email address (don't worry, we will discuss LEAD MAGNETS in great detail later). A lot of effort goes into a blog post, and its value shouldn't be spent after you publish it once online. Remember earlier when I mentioned MULTIFUNCTIONAL content? Always turn an initial effort into more by twice baking that sucker! Heck, quadruple-bake it!

FREE-BUT-NOT-FREE TRAFFIC SOURCE #3: PINTEREST

Contrary to what many people think, PINTEREST is not a social media platform. It is a search engine—very similar to Google. The search focus of Pinterest, though, is images. Pinterest is responsible for a HUGE share of the FREE traffic that comes to my blog at http://www.willowhavenoutdoor.com. I was shocked when I learned that. I always thought Pinterest was where people went to plan baby showers and look at shabby-chic ways to refurbish furniture. Boy, was I wrong!

Pinterest is totally free to use and quite simple to set up. Not only can you post your images and descriptions (with links back to your blog or YouTube channel) on Pinterest, but the readers of your blog can also post images that THEY like on their Pinterest accounts. With both Wordpress and Squarespace, it's very simple to make it so that all the images can be easily shared on Pinterest with one click. I manage my Pinterest account all from my phone while I'm waiting at the doctor's office, in line at the bank, waiting for a table in a crowded restaurant, etc.

There is definitely a strategy to posting on Pinterest. It's similar to the SEO concepts I discussed for blog posting previously. It does take a little bit

CHAPTER 6

of time to understand (I can teach you how to do it), but it's a FREE-BUT-NOT-FREE traffic source that everyone should consider.

FREE-BUT-NOT-FREE TRAFFIC SOURCE #4: INSTAGRAM & FACEBOOK

While I'm personally not a huge fan of building a business on the backs of social media platforms like INSTAGRAM & FACEBOOK, I've found them to be great supporting platforms for driving traffic to my blog, products, live courses, and online courses. These platforms are excellent places to post bits and pieces of the content you've created. They are great places for multifunctioning your blog content to gain additional reach and exposure. However, when you share your content on social media, it should be with purpose. When it comes to sharing your hard-earned content, there should be nothing random about it. Your entire goal is for someone to CLICK ON THAT CONTENT and end up on your REAL PLATFORM (a BLOG) so you can collect their email.

Creek's book,
SURVIVAL SLINGSHOTS.

One of Creek's
PINTEREST graphics.

YOUR ENTIRE GOAL IS FOR SOMEONE TO CLICK ON THAT CONTENT AND END UP ON YOUR REAL PLATFORM (A BLOG) SO YOU CAN COLLECT THEIR EMAIL.

Posting on social media reminds your customers that you exist, and if they see an excerpt or image that you've posted from a recent blog post or video, they may click it and visit your blog to read more. This will be an opportunity to either gather their email (if you don't already have it) OR display an advertisement of some kind to them for a product or service you offer. Better yet, you can have a CALL TO ACTION of some kind within your blog post. For example, I have a blog post about how to use Flint & Steel to start a fire. In that post, I feature a Flint & Steel Kit that I sell. Not only do I teach a reader how to use Flint & Steel (for FREE), but I also make an offer at the end for them to purchase my Flint & Steel Kit. For someone who doesn't have a Flint & Steel Kit, this is a no-brainer purchase if they want to practice at home. They've just seen me use it and know that it works well.

Whenever you post something on social media, there is always the chance that it will be shared by someone who sees it. For small business owners like you and me, these shares mean potential NEW IMPRESSIONS and NEW IMPRESSIONS mean NEW EMAILS. Ideally, some of these new impressions click on the links to your blog and become a part of your world. Better yet, you'll be able to collect some of their emails as well.

If you've done your research right and you've created blog content that answers questions and solves problems, you'll find that the reach of sharing these topics on social media will go much further than just random posts about your Smitch Niche or industry. People are always in the mood for good answers and solutions to problems they are facing. While they might not be actively searching for these topics on social media, as opposed to Google, your chances of getting their attention certainly improves.

FREE-BUT-NOT-FREE TRAFFIC SOURCE #5: BECOME A REGULAR CONTRIBUTOR TO AN INDUSTRY BLOG OR ONLINE MAGAZINE

This tactic is like GUEST POSTING, but the end goal is to become a regular weekly or monthly contributor. Also, instead of targeting blogs managed by individuals, you are targeting blogs managed by businesses. ALL industries these days have websites that operate like an online magazine and industry news outlet. ALL these websites use freelance writers to keep a constant flow of content streaming. These websites are completely dependent on fresh, new content in order to stay relevant. They know that content is the ONLY reason they exist. Whether these are online versions of actual print magazines or industry blogs, they all present a huge opportunity to anyone who is interested in getting in front of their readers and subscribers. It might take a little digging to find the Managing Editors of these websites, but all it takes is a simple email asking if they'd be interested in regular content about your NICHE TOPIC. I have a formula for almost ensuring your success in this that I'll share with you later if you'd like. Try to think outside of the box when pursuing this option. Don't pigeon-hole yourself into approaching ONLY sites that are directly related to your niche market. Rather, consider sites with a broader reach that have readers who may be interested in your niche topic. These blogs like to have a wide gamut of content and your ideas could be a perfect fit. Also, here's a **PRO TIP:** *Rather than accept a payment for contributing content, negotiate instead to include a byline with a link back to your own blog. You can make much more by building your email list and selling your own products and services. You can bet these potential blogs will want to see your own blog (or at least other content you've created) before considering you to contribute to their platform. I've been a contributor to a variety of websites over the years and have found this to be a very good traffic generator.*

FREE-BUT-NOT-FREE TRAFFIC SOURCE #6: YOUTUBE

YouTube is, without a doubt, one of the most powerful marketing tools the modern entrepreneur can utilize in today's online economy. It is also

CHAPTER 6

likely the most misunderstood, when it comes to generating sales. I can't tell you how many people I talk to who have started a YouTube channel in hopes of using it to generate revenue. When asked "HOW?" most of those people will reply something to the effect of, "Once I start getting enough views, then YouTube will start paying me money." While this is true, the number of videos and views necessary to generate a sizable amount of money from YouTube is far beyond what most channels will ever experience. Sadly, most YouTubers will spend exorbitant amounts of time, energy, and money—giving all their best skills, advice, and information away for free—and get nothing in return, except the feeling of being burnt out.

The HUGE misconception here is that YouTube is treated as THE BUSINESS instead of a marketing tool for AN ACTUAL BUSINESS.

Let's take my wilderness survival business, for example. Rather than creating wilderness survival videos in hopes that I will get views and then get paid by YouTube, it makes more sense to create videos that help to generate leads and facilitate the sale of the products and services that I offer within my actual Wilderness Survival Business. See what I mean? The end goal of these two scenarios is completely different. Ultimately, you must ask yourself, "Is YouTube my business, or do I use YouTube to market my business?"

The first is like buying a lottery ticket and hoping that you win, except it takes a whole heck of a lot more work. Being compensated for your time, effort, and energy is completely dependent on getting however many views YouTube deems necessary for you to earn something (this, by the way, changes all the time). Earning even a small amount of money requires an insane amount of views. Just to put this into perspective, I've screen captured the analytics from one of my YouTube channels below. This shows the data for the past year of activity. My videos have received approximately 406,700 views and I've earned $656.85, or $54.74/month. I guess it's better than nothing, but it is by no means a viable business in and of itself. At best, it's coffee money. After tithes and taxes, it's barely even that. It's certainly not worth the effort and energy that went into making the videos if that money was all I was getting. What's also important is that very few YouTubers will ever see half a million views in a year. I don't know the stats, but I'll bet my favorite survival knife that it's less than 1% of all channels get even that many views in a lifetime.

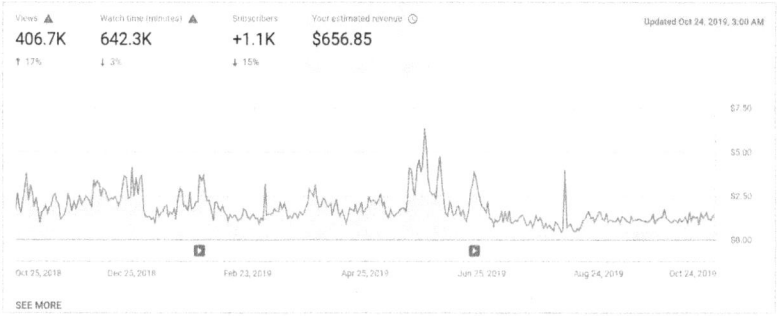

1-year analytics on one of Creek's YouTube channels.

Don't worry, I once thought this was how you made money with YouTube, too. Unfortunately, it took me way too long to figure out that it was a HORRIBLE business model for me. YouTube dangled the carrot and I chased it like a mindless donkey. I knew there had to be a better way.

TODAY—I EARN 1000s—maybe even 10s of 1000s of DOLLARS from YouTube each and every year.

HOW? Instead of giving all of my skills and expertise on a subject away for free in hopes of getting TONS OF VIEWS, I now give away strategic bits and pieces of my skills and expertise on a subject, in hopes of getting JUST A FEW VIEWS (tons of views is a bonus). I figured out that you can still teach something on YouTube and offer value to people without giving all your hard-earned knowledge away for free. I knew the knowledge that I had worked so many years to acquire was worth something. So, I changed my

CHAPTER 6

strategy. Today, my YouTube videos have ONE GOAL—to bring a viewer AWAY from YouTube and ONTO my own platform where I have a chance at gathering their email. YouTube owns my YouTube Subscriber list, not me. I own my email list, not YouTube. I prefer the latter. YouTube helps me grow my email list with targeted and qualified leads, which I use to sell my products and services. I still monetize my videos but certainly don't depend on that income for anything more than the gumball machine on the way out of the local grocery store.

Screencapture of one of Creek's YouTube videos. The link in the video description is designed to pull someone away from YouTube.

TODAY, MY YOUTUBE VIDEOS HAVE ONE GOAL—TO BRING A VIEWER AWAY FROM YOUTUBE AND ONTO MY OWN PLATFORM WHERE I HAVE A CHANCE AT GATHERING THEIR EMAIL.

CHAPTER 6

Everyone with a product or service to sell can use this exact strategy. I'll give you a real-life example: I recently filmed a video about the PERFECT Bow Drill Technique and uploaded it to YouTube. In the video, I show the exact technique I've mastered over the past 20 years for making a fire using the Bow Drill. It's a seriously valuable video to someone searching the internet about how to use the Bow Drill. ***BUT I don't just stop there and hope I get a lot of views and eventually a check from YouTube.*** I include a link in the description box for my FREE Bow Drill Carving Template and also some FREE Bow Drill Wood Identification Guides. These are both very valuable downloads to someone who is trying to figure out how to start a fire using the Bow Drill. When a viewer clicks on that link, all they must do is enter their email to get it. I then enter that person into an email automation that delivers them the downloads. I also invite them to take my in-depth online course that I sell, which details how to carve and make a Bow Drill Kit. THIS is how you use YouTube to make money and gather leads for FREE. I'll fill you in on the rest of the process throughout the upcoming chapters of this book.

The great thing about YouTube videos is that you can embed them into your BLOG platform as well. You can write a blog post that summarizes the video and then use the video to provide additional value to the reader. Your videos should work as standalone marketing tools on YouTube AND as supplemental material on your BLOG. When they're shared on social media outlets, online communities, and linked to on PINTEREST, they have even more potential to drive traffic.

FINAL THOUGHTS

If you invest time into your blog and create KILLER CONTENT that is grounded in good research and SEO principles, and if you're following the genuine and authentic grass-roots methods I've outlined about using online forums, groups, social sites, blogs, and YouTube videos, then you WILL start to attract your ideal and perfect audience. How you handle these potential

CHAPTER 6

customers is the most important thing you'll ever do in your business. It's even more important than the product(s) you sell or will sell in the future. What's done with this traffic separates those who do this for a HOBBY and those who do this to MAKE A LIVING!

CHAPTER 7: PILLAR # 4: BUILDING YOUR EMAIL LIST

There is a HIGH probability that once someone visits your blog through a search engine link or external online blurb, such as a YouTube video, they will never return. It's not personal. Consumers in the digital age, are bombarded with all kinds of media. There are literally 1000s of brands, businesses, and blogs vying for their attention 24 hours a day, 365 days a year. Even if someone visits your blog and says to themselves, "I love this blog. I'm definitely going to come back here when I'm not driving or when I get out of the doctor's office or when I get a break at work," it's likely they will never return. They simply forget about you.

This is a MAJOR issue for us small business entrepreneurs. They were interested enough in your content and your subject matter to click over in the first place. If this is the only chance you have to solve their problems and don't have a way to capture their email, then you're screwed, and you might as well join the millions of people who have tried to start a business (part-time or full-time) online and failed. There are only 2 options at this point:

1. Retarget that visitor with a Facebook Pixel Ad, which requires paying money (and doesn't get their email)

2. Get their email so that you can get back in touch with them

YOU MUST MAKE EVERY EFFORT POSSIBLE TO GET A POTENTIAL CUSTOMER'S EMAIL AS SOON AS SOON AS THEY VISIT YOUR PLATFORM!

CHAPTER 7

When visitors trade their email address for something on your blog, they become part of your internal list. *YOU OWN THIS LIST.* You now have a way to get back in touch with each visitor and remind them about you, your content, and your services. You now have a vehicle to continue to answer their questions and solve their problems, and you have a way to nurture a relationship with them. Thus, you have a fighting chance of converting them into a paying customer.

My blogs and websites these days are loaded with a variety of ways to convince visitors to give me their email. I currently use the email software at http://www.activecampaign.com, but I've also used http://www.mailchimp.com. There are tons of email management software providers in the marketplace. These are just the two I have used and like.

At their most basic level, these services allow you to create a little input form that says, "SUBSCRIBE TO MY BLOG." Then, this form can be quickly and easily integrated it into your website. When someone visits your blog and enters their email to SUBSCRIBE, then they become a part of your internal list, which you can email anytime you want.

UNFORTUNATELY—this is where 90% of people who are desperately trying to build a business using online traffic stop. The HARSH TRUTH is that only a FRACTION of people will voluntarily subscribe to someone's blog or channel. Subscribing to a blog or "newsletter" used to be a novel thing, but now it's old hat and no one does it. Asking someone to subscribe to your blog is the absolute bare minimum you can do when it comes to gathering emails and, quite frankly, it's archaic and lazy. Don't take it personally if you're currently operating this way. I'm trying to help!

Just subscribing to your blog doesn't provide a visitor with VALUE, and it certainly doesn't help solve their problems. It doesn't give them anything. They need to be wooed and motivated to become a customer. They need to be convinced with something valuable, enticing, and IMMEDIATE! They want SOLUTIONS!

There are 100s of more creative ways to ask your visitors for their email address, and additional input forms can be generated for each one of them through one of the email providers I've mentioned. The best way to convince a potential customer to give you their email is to trade them something. This FREE "something" is called a LEAD MAGNET. I say "something" because a Lead Magnet can take on many different forms.

A **"LEAD MAGNET"** is the marketing phrase for the product, download, or service you're using to trade for someone's email. You're enticing them **(the LEAD)** with something **(the MAGNET)**.

Before I get into some LEAD MAGNET examples, let's first discuss the key properties of a good Lead Magnet:

- **It's FREE:** While I've done low-priced Lead Magnets, conversion is MUCH HIGHER when the Lead Magnet doesn't cost your blog visitor anything. People love FREE things.
- **It's IMMEDIATE:** We live in a society where everyone wants it NOW. You must deliver your Lead Magnet to your visitor immediately. Also, getting it cannot be complicated. Don't make visitors jump through any weird hoops.
- **It's SPECIFIC:** I've found that the more specific your Lead Magnet can be, the better. It should directly relate to either answering the immediate questions or solving the immediate problems of your ideal customer.

- **It has a high PERCEIVED VALUE:** Ideally, your Lead Magnet is valuable to your potential customers. The higher the perceived value, the higher the conversions (how many people give you their email for it). By the way, if your Lead Magnet solves a problem for your audience, it's already valuable.
- **It's SHORT & SWEET:** Yes, it's possible to deliver something of value that's also easy for the visitor to consume. I've found that short and concise Lead Magnets convert better than some massive book or report. There are always exceptions to this, but if you're just developing your first Lead Magnet, make it a short one. You can always get more elaborate once you get the hang of the process.

Here is a list of examples I have used over the years that work well (I'm sure you'll be able to think of even more):

- **CHEAT SHEET:** Help them get to where they want to be by giving them the steps in an easy-to-follow Cheat Sheet format.
- **WATCH A SPECIAL VIDEO:** Create a hidden page on your blog where you teach or show something using a video. Tease this exclusive FREE training on your blog homepage and require visitors to enter their email address in order to access it.
- **SOLVE A SPECIFIC PROBLEM:** Lead Magnets that solve problems are email list gold.
- **LEARN A SPECIAL SKILL:** Create a hidden page on your blog where you teach a special skill that your audience might want to learn. Tease this exclusive, FREE training on your blog homepage and require visitors to enter their email address in order to access it.

CHAPTER 7

Exclusive video training on Creek's APOCABOX website—a user must enter their email to receive a link to watch the subscriber-only video.

- **Give away a FREE book, PDF, or manual.** Tease this FREE download on your blog homepage and require visitors to enter their email addresses so you can email them the FREE download link (THIS ONE IS VERY POPULAR).

- **BLOG POST INTEGRATIONS:** If someone is reading (and liking) one of your blog posts, it only makes sense to try and capture their email in that moment. I like to drop email sign-up forms right in the middle of my most popular blog posts. If the reader likes your content, then they will likely subscribe so they can be alerted when you post new content. A Lead Magnet that helps a reader take the NEXT STEP while reading a blog post is a good one. For example, in my blog post about How to Start A Fire with the Bow Drill, I offer a FREE Downloadable Carving Template. This allows the reader to take the NEXT STEP after reading the blog post.

99

CHAPTER 7

- **DISCOUNT CODES:** If you sell products, you can tell visitors that if they enter their email address you will INSTANTLY email them a 10%-off coupon code, which they can immediately apply to their order. I'm sure you've experienced this before while shopping online. This one doesn't necessarily solve problems but it's a good way to get emails and build your list.

- **CALENDAR:** People love when you map out a plan for them. Almost any expert can create a calendar for their market. For example, I once created a "FOOD STORAGE CALENDAR" that mapped out a 30-DAY PLAN for storing food and water in anticipation of a large-scale disaster. It was one of my most successful email collectors to date. I see people in the diet and fitness industry use this strategy as well (example: 30-Day Meal Plan for Going Keto). I also have a WILD FORAGING CALENDAR that someone can download on my site http://www.wildedibleplantofthemonth.com.

Creek's Wild Edible Plant of the Month Club website where someone must enter their email to receive a FREE Wild Foraging Calendar.

- **PRINTABLE CHECKLIST:** Checklists make fantastic Lead Magnets. One of the best checklist Lead Magnets I've ever used that was ultra-specific to my niche was a "BUG OUT BAG SHOPPING LIST: A Checklist for Everything You Need to Pack in Your Bug Out Bag." I typed out the list in a Microsoft Word document and hired someone on FIVERR.COM for $8 to turn it into an awesome downloadable PDF checklist.

- **AUDIO DOWNLOAD:** Recording an MP3 audio file on your phone is simple these days. Most phones even have a built-in sound recorder app. Pick a hot topic within your industry and record a 15 minute "PODCAST" that you then offer as a FREE download when someone visits your site. I once recorded myself reading Jack London's short story "TO BUILD A FIRE" and offered it as a FREE download and you wouldn't believe how many people traded their email for it!

- **A QUIZ:** A free quiz is quite possibly one of the best converting Lead Magnets on the planet. A great place to have quizzes made is https://www.qzzr.com/. Here are a few quick examples:

    - Would you survive the APOCALYPSE? Take this short quiz to find out!
    - What kind of a driver are you? Take this 30-second quiz to find out!
    - Are you datable? Take the DATE ME QUIZ and find out!

- **A CHALLENGE:** I've found a 5-DAY CHALLENGE to be a fantastic Lead Magnet. I recently implemented what I call the 5-DAY BUG OUT BAG CHALLENGE on one of my websites. When someone lands on the homepage, they can enter their email to sign up for the FREE 5-DAY CHALLENGE where I teach them how to build a Bug Out Bag and challenge them to follow along at home to get their own put together as well. It is proving to be one of the most successful Lead Magnets I've ever used. I can also post this challenge on social media and even make a YouTube video for it to help drive even more traffic and grow my email list. A challenge Lead Magnet like this should HELP your market solve a problem and give them

CHAPTER 7

quick, concise steps for getting it done. A challenge Lead Magnet is the perfect transition to offering your leads a more elaborate training about your subject. For example, after someone takes my 5-Day Bug Out Bag Challenge, I invite them to take my online course titled Build the Perfect Bug Out Bag, where we dig into the subject in much more detail, which includes teaching many survival skills. The challenge is a free, valuable teaser that showcases your knowledge as an instructor and helps your customer become engaged. I'm currently building out a 5-Day Wild Edible Plant Challenge for my Wild Edible Plant of the Month Club business where I invite people to learn 5 of the most common wild edible plants. Afterwards, I'll invite them to become a member of Wild Edible Plant of the Month Club. Do you see where I'm heading here?

Notice the email form at my blog, willowhavenoutdoor.com, where a visitor can receive a FREE copy of my Pocket Field Guide titled Survival Tarp Shelters.

I want you to take a few minutes and brainstorm some other potential ideas for getting a visitor's email. List some specific products, trainings, or information that customers in your Smitch Niche would gladly trade their email for. What problems can you solve with a FREE Lead Magnet? Be creative but try to stick with one of the examples mentioned!

CHAPTER 7

Each time a visitor enters their email, they can be added to a specific list that you create within your email provider, or they can receive what's called a TAG, which is just another way of organizing your email addresses and lists. You can create lists or tags for different things. For example, I have a list that is specific to visitors who have entered giveaways, a list for visitors who have subscribed while reading a blog post about fire-starting, a list for visitors who have requested access to a particular video training, and a list for visitors who wish to watch one of my free webinars. I have specific lists for specific visitors and my communication with each list is different. For the visitors who subscribed while reading a fire-starting-related blog post, I send them messages, initially, about fire-starting skills and invite them to take some fire training with me or offer them some of my fire-starting products. For visitors who have subscribed to watch a free webinar about how to build a Bug Out Bag, I email them with content related to Bug Out Bags and disaster preparedness. I'm sure you're starting to see how powerful this approach can be. It allows you to hone-in and deliver content that you KNOW your visitors want and offer them products and services that DIRECTLY relate to that content.

CHAPTER 7

THE RELATIONSHIP MUST WORK FOR YOU (THE CREATOR)

You see, most blog posts, Instagram posts, or YouTube videos don't require any kind of commitment from the reader. They're free nuggets of information for anyone who lands on your page. For the purposes of building a business, this relationship doesn't ultimately work for us (the business owners), does it? We need a commitment from the reader, or at least some of them. We need them to give us something. Ultimately, it would be nice if they would trade us dollars for something of value that we sell—a product. Before that, though, we want their email. We've got their attention, now we want their email—as fast as we can possibly get it!

When someone gives you their email in exchange for something, your relationship with them changes. They have transitioned from a non-committal reader to a very interesting prospect. If you don't get their email, then you'll probably have no hope of selling anything to them. This task is very likely the single most important job for your blog or YouTube channel AND YOUR BUSINESS!

As I've already detailed, one of my best capture methods for getting a visitor's email is to require it in order to receive a FREE download of some kind. Below is a really great way to produce content for your blog or channel and slowly build a valuable, downloadable piece of content that you can use to barter for a prospect's email, in addition to the ones I listed above. This method kills two birds with one stone.

YOUR FIRST DOWNLOADABLE MANUAL (FOR FREE OR EVEN PAID)

I want you to think of something that would be incredibly valuable to someone within your Smitch Niche market. In my wilderness survival business, for example, it might be something like how to start a fire with the bow drill, how to store survival food for a large-scale natural disaster, or how to identify wild edible plants. Choose a specific topic that would interest people within your Smitch Niche that also SOLVES A PROBLEM or TEACHES SOMETHING. Do your research to make sure they are actually searching for this! I can show you how to do this later.

Then, I want you to break that topic down into a few blog posts. If you can't teach everything about the topic in 3–5 average-size blog posts or less, then choose a smaller, more manageable topic. Next, I want you to write those blog posts and post them to your site. It may take a while, and that's fine. Don't try to write them all in one afternoon. MAKE THEM GOOD. Take lots of photos where applicable. Try to make these some of your best posts to date. By the time you're done, you will have an outstanding piece of content with several short chapters teaching a topic of interest to an average person within your Smitch Niche.

These blog posts now comprise your first self-published manual. I want you to compile those into a digital PDF. You may want to write short introduction and conclusion sections, if these aren't already present in your blog posts. You can lay them out yourself in Microsoft Word or a Desktop Publishing program, such as CorelDraw and simply save or print to a PDF. Be sure to include all those great photos in the PDF, too! If you're not comfortable with desktop publishing, there are other options, such as https://www.fiverr.com/, where you can hire freelance designers to do it for you at reasonable rates. I've used Fiverr for many projects over the years and have always had great results. In fact, here is an "inside link" to 20% off your first order with Fiverr, should you ever need to use their service: http://www.fiverr.com/s2/4a8b4c785a (If you use this link, I get a kickback. It's called an affiliate link. Affiliate links are also a way you can earn money on your blog).

Fiverr.com is also a great place to hire someone to design your book cover. All good books, whether print or digital, need a good book cover. It's

CHAPTER 7

the cover, I've found, that ultimately sells the book!

Once you have this new self-published PDF manual, I want you to delete all those posts from your blog, except for the first one.

Next, I want you to edit that first blog post so that at the bottom it reads something like this:

"Want to dig deeper into this subject? Enter your email below, and I'll send you my FREE 47-page digital e-book titled "HOW TO......."

Or, you can feature this FREE download on your homepage with a message like this:

"FREE 47-PAGE E-BOOK DOWNLOAD: THE ULTIMATE GUIDE TO _____! Enter your email for an instant FULL MANUSCRIPT download link!"

You can also update your social media profiles to mention your free resource. If you've done your homework and know what your market wants, people WILL click on it! And, you WILL start to build your list.

Do you see where I'm going with this? You now have a valuable piece of content that some people might even pay for! However, you're going to give it away for FREE in exchange for your reader's email. Who knows, maybe one day you'll even decide to sell it?

I sell 1000s of little printed guides (that I call Pocket Field Guides) each year that were all developed from successful blog posts. Here's a screen capture for the past 30-days of just 5 of them. Most of these sell passively through Amazon.com and I never see them.

CHAPTER 7

 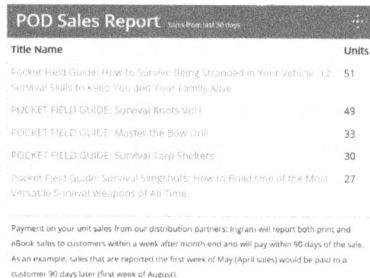

Screen capture of last 30-day sales for just 5 of Creek's printed guides that were developed from successful blog posts.

MORAL OF THE STORY: Your blog posts can be fleshed out into REAL BOOKS and used to generate PASSIVE INCOME for you and your family for generations to come.

How valuable should my LEAD MAGNET be?

I'm often asked how valuable a LEAD MAGNET should be? In my opinion, a good LEAD MAGNET is one of the most important things you can have. It's almost solely responsible for getting emails from potential customers. Your LEAD MAGNET should be IRRESISTIBLE! Selling to a total stranger the 1st time they visit your platform is very difficult. Often-times, your only chance of converting them to a paying

CHAPTER 7

customer is to capture their email. Thus, the value of your LEAD MAGNET is PRICELESS.

Bottom line—make your LEAD MAGNET a good one. Make it look good, too (this means hiring a designer to polish it up)! You will be judged by the quality of your Lead Magnet, and it will be a reflection of the quality of products or services your prospects will eventually buy from you. MAKE IT GOOD!

Ask yourself what your market would pay for, then give them that for FREE (in exchange for their email, of course)!

This self-published manual, compiled from the blog posts mentioned, can also become your PLATFORM for promotion. You now have a BOOK! Sure, it's small, but it's still a book. And every "expert" should have a book to use for marketing and promotion. EVERY expert. EVERY EXPERT.

One of the most amazing features available through current email providers is that ALL I've just described can be set up to be delivered automatically—24/7/365. When someone requests your LEAD MAGNET, your email provider can respond automatically—even WHILE YOU SLEEP! You create the emails once and let the software do the rest. Don't worry, it's not hard. The automation side of this concept is what really took my business to a whole new level!

You're probably starting to wonder how and when all this work converts to dollars. After all, you are running a business, right? Fair enough, let's talk about a concept I call "give COLD, sell WARM."

CHAPTER 8: PILLAR # 5: THE CUSTOMER ON-RAMP

I have a phrase— **"Give COLD, Sell WARM."**

Let me paint a picture for you:

You're walking down the street and a total stranger walks up to you and tries to sell you a book. They talk for a few seconds about how much they like it and are adamant that you will like it, too. Then, they ask for your credit card. Do you think you'd buy that book? If you said yes, then I'd probably call you crazy. No person in their right mind is going to buy a book under those circumstances.

Now, imagine this:

You've attended an event with a friend. You're hearing an expert speak about a topic you and your buddy are both interested in. You know a little bit about the speaker, but your buddy is a raving fan and has nothing but great things to say about him. You arrive a little early and, as you walk into the room, someone who works for the speaker explains that if you subscribe to their email list, then you can get a voucher for a free cup of coffee to enjoy during the speech. You do so without even thinking much of it, and she quickly enters your email using the iPad in her hands and gives you the voucher. While you're waiting in your seat, enjoying your free cup of coffee, your phone dings. It's a new email from the speaker! He thanks you for attending the event and tells you a quick and entertaining story about how he got into this line of work. Between your buddy, the free coffee, and this story, you're really starting to like this guy. After the speech, which you find very insightful and helpful, you approach the speaker's table at the back of

CHAPTER 8

the room. He thanks you for coming, shakes your hand, and asks if you'd like to buy one of his books. Do you think you'd buy that book? Yes, you probably would. Not only because your buddy vouches for him, but also because he gave a great talk that you really enjoyed. He added value to your day. Heck, you'd probably ask him to sign the book, too!

The difference between these two scenarios is night and day. When it comes to selling whatever product, service, or training you have to offer to your visitors, DON'T be the weird stranger walking up to people on the street, instantly trying to sell them something! This is the difference between COLD and WARM traffic. Customers should always have the opportunity to purchase a product or service, if they wish, on their first visit to your platform, but the underlying strategy is to be prepared in case they don't! And trust me, most of them will leave without buying.

When visitors first click over to your blog, they're most likely COLD traffic. They probably don't know you. They likely don't trust you yet. They may have never even heard of you before! It's doubtful they have friends who will vouch for you. Essentially, you and your first-time visitors are STRANGERS in every sense of the word. FOR THE LOVE OF ALL THAT IS GOOD, don't let them leave without getting their email! Like I said, there should be ways to purchase products and services from your blog or platform should they choose to do so when they first arrive, but we're going to save the real selling for a little bit later.

Your first job is to collect their email. Your second job is to convert them from COLD traffic to WARM traffic. The best way to do this is to give them value, answer their questions, and solve their problems—ideally, for FREE. My phrase "give COLD, sell WARM" should start making sense now. Giving COLD and selling WARM is a simple way of saying you need to BUILD A RELATIONSHIP with your customer.

I know how tempting it can be to try to sell someone something right out of the gate. I've made that mistake too many times to count. It rarely

CHAPTER 8

(if ever) works. Most customers aren't in a rush to immediately purchase what you have to sell and very likely haven't come to your site with the intention of buying anything, anyway (unless you're an ER doctor or plumber who fixes busted water pipes). It's easy to get excited about your product or service. But, just because YOU'RE excited, doesn't mean ANYONE ELSE is. In fact, I'll pretty much guarantee that no one else is. Sorry, but it's true. Your job is to get your potential customers excited and take them on a journey through your sales process, often called a "sales funnel."

One of the best ways to convert potential customers from COLD traffic to WARM traffic is through a series of emails immediately after they give you their email and download your Lead Magnet. You must strike while the iron is hot, as they say. They have given you their email because they like something you had to offer. And, they might even like you. It's now time to nurture that interest and start to develop a real relationship with them. Remember, behind EVERY email address is a REAL PERSON with problems, concerns, and a REAL LIFE. I can't express the importance of this initial phase of communication.

Before we get into the details, I need to remind you of something—your visitors gave you their email because of what you or your Lead Magnet could possibly do for THEM. They are only interested in what YOU or YOUR BLOG can do for THEM. Never try to turn the table and make this about YOU. All your focus should revolve around what YOU can do for THEM. Lead with service and value and the rest will take care of itself. You'll be tempted to make this about YOU, because you're excited to sell some stuff, but please proceed with patience, self-discipline, and trust the process. The sooner you realize that (MOST) customers are only in this for themselves, the better.

At its core, a well-crafted CUSTOMER ON-RAMP EMAIL SERIES will nurture a relationship with your potential (or current) customer while simultaneously freeing up your most valuable asset—YOUR TIME. I've written and automated more on-ramp email campaigns than I could possibly count. I'm constantly testing new campaigns and revising old ones.

The first thing a customer on-ramp should do is DELIVER ON THE PROMISE of your Lead Magnet. If you've followed the plan so far, a potential customer has given you their email in exchange for something (a FREE LEAD MAGNET). Thus, you need to get their FREE THING to them as fast and as easy possible. Don't overcomplicate this step. Just send them an email with access to the Lead Magnet, say Thank You, and tell them you'll follow up with them in a few days.

From there, the approach all depends on the products and services you hope to offer in the coming days. I've found great success in TEACHING and SOLVING PROBLEMS that relate to the topic of the Lead Magnet the customer requested. You can never go wrong with TEACHING someone something—EVER. When you teach, you build trust and authority. In my opinion, there is no better way to lead a customer to a sale than to teach them something that relates to the Lead Magnet they chose to receive.

Whether you sell physical goods, digital goods, books, online courses, live courses, or anything between, teaching can be the bridge that leads a customer from the Lead Magnet to the purchase of your products or services. I call this part of the Customer On-Ramp THE TEACHING BRIDGE. It is also a really great way to eliminate being salesy. Let me give you three really great examples from my own business:

EXAMPLE # 1:
The end goal is to sell my online Bow Drill Building Course.

LEAD MAGNET:
Bow Drill Carving Template with opt-in embedded into a blog post titled How to Make Fire Using the Bow Drill

TEACHING BRIDGE:
I send them a free training video about how to master Bow Drill Technique.

PITCH:
Now that they know the technique, I offer to teach them how to MAKE their own kit for $15.95 via an online course.

EXAMPLE # 2:
The end goal is to sell my book titled THE NONCON PACK.

LEAD MAGNET:
An offer to download a FREE chapter (the FIRE CHAPTER) of my book.

TEACHING BRIDGE:
I send a few emails that point out a few critical pieces of the FIRE CHAPTER that they have, using them as teaching moments.

PITCH:
They've had an opportunity to read the FIRE CHAPTER, now they can get the whole book on Amazon for $21.95.

EXAMPLE # 3:
The end goal is to sell my online fire-starting class THE ART OF FIRE.

LEAD MAGNET:
A video teaching my favorite fire-starting skill—I teach how to use a credit card-sized Fresnel lens to start fires and offer to give potential customers one for FREE if they send me a self-addressed stamped envelope.

TEACHING BRIDGE:
The teaching bridge here is also the Lead Magnet.

PITCH:
Do they like survival fire-starting?
Take my 10-week ART OF FIRE Course for $98.

CHAPTER 8

It doesn't matter what your product is, I believe there is a LEAD MAGNET and TEACHING BRIDGE combination that can help you (automatically) lead a potential customer to a sale.

This is why I love FREE TRAININGS and FREE CHALLENGES so much. It combines the Lead Magnet, the Teaching Bridge, and the On-Ramp Emails all into one awesome package. Take my 5-DAY BUG OUT BAG CHALLENGE below for example:

5-DAY BUG OUT BAG CHALLENGE:
The end goal is to sell my online Bug Out Bag Building Course.
LEAD MAGNET:
5-DAY Bug Out Bag Challenge: 5 emails for 5 days delivering links to free Bug Out Bag training videos. I have these opt-ins on my website and embedded into blog articles I've written on the subject.
. TEACHING BRIDGE:
For 5 days, I teach about how to build a Bug Out Bag with links in the 5 daily on-ramp emails.
PITCH:
To take Bug Out Bag skills further, I offer an online course for $32.95.

In this challenge I teach the basics of building a 72-hour disaster survival kit. I give a ton of great information away for FREE to someone who's interested in building out their own kit. At the end of the 5-day challenge, I invite them to take their training to the next level with my online course. Many of the people who take the challenge end up taking my online course. Let's break down what happens during this 5-day challenge email on-ramp series:

1. I deliver some valuable training for FREE

2. Potential customers get to learn from me and learn what kind of a teacher I am, without making any kind of commitment

3. I deliver value and solve a problem (help them get started building their own Bug Out Bag)

4. I build trust and authority on the subject

5. The natural next step is to take more training from me—except the next level training isn't free

In fact, roughly 20% of the people who take that challenge end up enrolling in the advanced course for $32.95. Everyone who remains subscribed (some will unsubscribe from my email list for one reason or another) will continue to receive regular emails from me moving forward. Some of those emails will give updates or offer free tutorials and others will be offers for products, services, online courses, webinars, field courses, etc. Many of those people will buy other products or services in the future. The point is that I can contact these interested prospects over and over (unless they unsubscribe), and it costs me nothing except the monthly email host fee. This allows me to maximize what's called "the lifetime value" of a customer. I don't want to be a one-hit-wonder when it comes to sales. My goal is to develop a relationship with my customers and try to solve multiple problems for them for years to come!

At this point, you're probably chomping at the bit to get started on your own, but I have more to tell you!

Creek's BugOut Bag Course at OutdoorCore.com

CHAPTER 8

ADVANCED WEBINAR APPROACH

    Besides building credibility and trust using email, I've found that a free webinar can be a fantastic way to do the same. A webinar is basically just a video, except it's made specifically to teach something. A free webinar can function as BOTH a Lead Magnet AND a customer on-ramp, simultaneously. For example, I have a free webinar called 12 THINGS YOU DIDN'T KNOW YOU NEEDED IN YOUR BUG OUT BAG. You can sign up to watch it on my website—all you have to do is enter your email. When you do, I send you the link to view the video. In this video, I spend 1 hour teaching about these 12 items. I also tell the viewer my story and do my best to build trust and credibility by offering up tons of knowledge about building out a Bug Out Bag. A video effort like this can easily warm up a cold lead. By the end, you've shared your expertise and potentially even solved a problem for them. This is a great opportunity to invite them to take an online course, sign-up for a live training, or even consider purchasing your book or other physical products. I've successfully used this approach many times and it allows you to get to a sale a more quickly than a 1–2-week email on-ramp.

CHAPTER 8

A FEW MORE EXAMPLES

A straightforward Lead Magnet example is on my website at http://www.myapocabox.com. APOCABOX is my subscription survival box. Here, I give visitors an opportunity to watch a 30-minute subscriber exclusive video. For access, however, they must give me their email. When they do, my email provider automatically sends them the video link (I set this up in advance, of course). Then, I send them a series of emails that ends with a special offer to subscribe to APCOABOX.

I also use a Lead Magnet at my website http://www.wildedibleplantofthemonth.com. This is a monthly subscription service where I teach about Wild Edible Plants. For this Lead Magnet, I offer a free Wild Foraging Calendar. In order to receive the download, a visitor must first give me their email. When they do, I immediately send them (automatically, 24/7) the download link and then, over the course of the next several days, tell them my background with wild edible plants and how I developed a system for studying them in which they may be interested. The email series ends with an offer to subscribe to my monthly subscription service.

The Lead Magnet at my main website, http://www.creekstewart.com, is an offer to watch a FREE training video that ends with instructions about how to get my favorite fire-starting tool for FREE. When someone gives me their email, I immediately (automatically, of course) send them the video link. The video describes how to use a wallet-sized magnifying glass to start a fire and then tells the viewer to send me a self-addressed stamped envelope, and I will mail them one for FREE. We receive at least 50 self-addressed stamped envelopes every week at my office. I mail them information about my other services along with the FREE magnifying glass.

I also offer FREE PREVIEWS for my online courses at http://www.outdoorcore.com. Can you guess what the visitor needs to do before they can view them? Yes, enter their email.

CHAPTER 8

I have Lead Magnets everywhere. That's because my #1 marketing objective for my business is to gather the emails of potential customers. It's the best way I've found to "on-ramp" a customer into my world. I am also convinced that a deliberate effort to collect emails and use them to quickly develop relationships with your customers is the single most important aspect of being successful with an online-driven business today. EVERYONE goes online to find products and services. In fact, EVERYONE uses the internet, in some way, for almost EVERYTHING. If you want to be in business or are already in business, then developing your Lead Magnet(s), implementing an email collector, and writing an "on-ramp" email series should be at the very top of your priority list—even before product development. Heck, your email subscribers can tell you exactly what they want you to sell them! Just email them and ask!

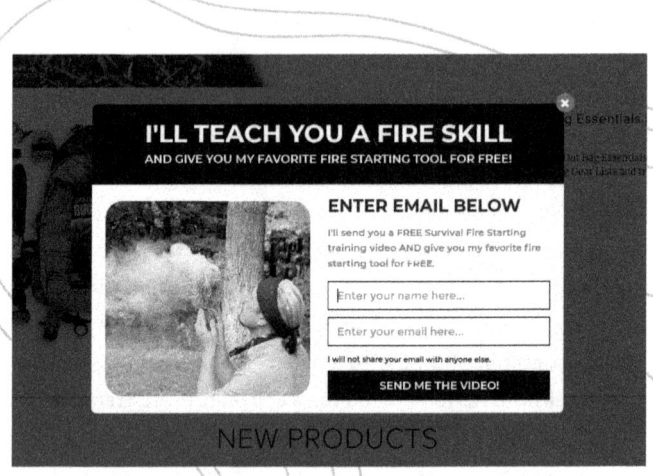

Lead Magnet pop-up at creekstewart.com

CHAPTER 9: SURVIVAL SNARE EMAIL COLLECTOR

When I discuss trapping in my wilderness survival courses, I always mention how snares and traps make a lot of sense because once they are set, they continue to work passively, gathering food for you while you can focus on other survival priorities, such as shelter, water, and fire. A snare works passively, 24/7, to secure your meals as opposed to "active hunting," which is a major time suck that consumes valuable calories and energy.

EVERY BUSINESS NEEDS A "SURVIVAL SNARE" ON THEIR WEBSITE OR BLOG.

CHAPTER 9

The parallels between survival trapping and selling your products and services are off the charts! Every business needs a "survival snare" on their website or blog. EVERY BUSINESS. The "survival snare" that works 24/7 for you is, of course, the LEAD MAGNET and EMAIL COLLECTOR working together. The LEAD MAGNET is the BAIT and the EMAIL COLLECTOR is the SNARE. They work together passively, around the clock, gathering emails, giving customers value, and taking them through your on-ramp email series to build trust and establish credibility in your Smitch Niche. During this process, they learn about how you got to where you are, why you're doing what you do, and hopefully how your product or service might solve a problem for them (or at least have a positive influence in their life). And, ideally, you're building trust every step of the way by teaching them something. You are turning complete strangers into customers through the power of teaching! And, the best part is that it's all done automatically!

YOU ARE TAKING YOUR CUSTOMERS on a journey into your business!

In this chapter I want to get into the details about the "email collector" portion of this process. First, it's important that you understand every step in the entire on-ramp process, from when your prospective customer enters their email to when they receive their offer, is done automatically. In the email marketing world, this is called an AUTOMATION, and any email marketing service/platform worth its salt will have AUTOMATION as a feature.

An automated email campaign is one that starts with what's called a TRIGGER. A trigger is simply an event, like when someone signs up for your email list because they want to receive your free LEAD MAGNET. Once the trigger happens, the automated email campaign takes over and automatically sends out a series of prewritten emails, according to the schedule you create. Then, once the campaign is over, the customer remains on your email list for you to contact with regular updates, as you please (unless they unsubscribe, of course).

Without the automation portion of this equation, none of what I've told you is feasible. It is virtually impossible to do this process manually. And, it would be so time consuming that it wouldn't make any sense—you could never be available 24/7 to send the necessary information in a timely manner that would be satisfactory to your customer. THIS PROCESS MUST BE AUTOMATED, and it is this technology that has changed the marketing landscape for boot-strap entrepreneurs like you and me.

Just because the email campaign is set up to be automatic doesn't mean you're off the hook when it comes to responding to emails. Many customers will REPLY to your automated email series with comments and questions. All these replies should receive a personalized response from you or your team. This really helps to develop the relationship and makes an automated campaign even more impactful.

CHAPTER 9

Below is the basic step-by-step process for setting up a successful lead-generating automated email on-ramp campaign:

CREATE THE LEAD MAGNET

CREATE A NEW LIST INSIDE OF YOUR EMAIL MARKETING PLATFORM (this is simply your in-house email list that your new prospects will be on)

CREATE THE EMAIL SIGN UP FORM IN YOUR MARKETING EMAIL PLATFORM AND ASSIGN IT TO THE LIST ABOVE
(copy the embed code for this form)

DECIDE WHERE ON YOUR BLOG/WEBSITE YOU WANT TO OFFER THE LEAD MAGNET AND HOW

INTEGRATE THE EMBED CODE (provided by your marketing email provider) **ON THAT PAGE**

CREATE AN AUTOMATED EMAIL CAMPAIGN and ON-RAMP SEQUENCE WITHIN YOUR EMAIL MARKETING PLATFORM WITH THE START TRIGGER BEING WHEN A CUSTOMER SIGNS UP FOR THE EMAIL LIST ABOVE

RESPOND TO ANY COMMENTS, FEEDBACK, ETC.

CHAPTER 9

Even though these steps are simple, I know that the overall process can seem a bit overwhelming to tackle by yourself. However, I promise it is very easy and anyone, with any level of computer or internet knowledge, can do it. I'll also give you a unique opportunity, a little later, to "look over my shoulder" and show you exactly how I do it in my own business.

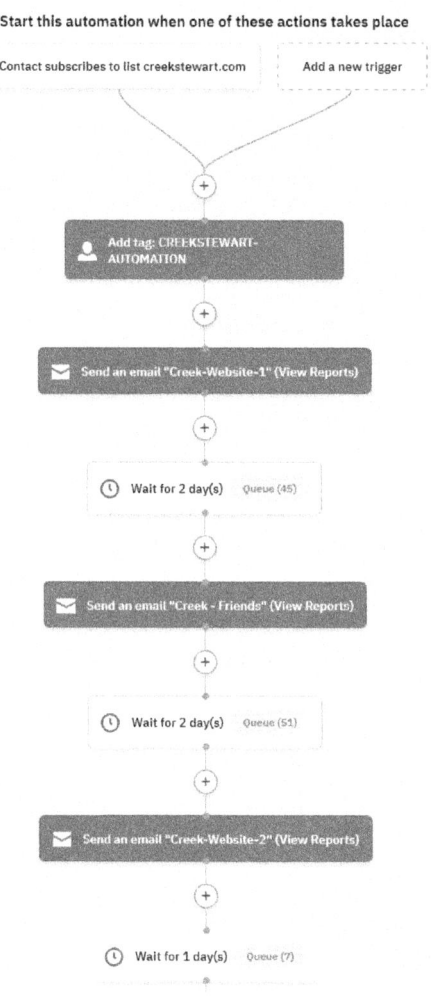

One of Creek's email automations (what it looks like on the backend).

CHAPTER 10: A PRODUCT EVERY "EXPERT" SHOULD CONSIDER

If you are trying to build a business around your area of expertise (I don't care if you're a climber, spoon carver, wild forager, trail runner, fishing enthusiast, pottery teacher, or a WILDERNESS SURVIVAL INSTRUCTOR), then I have something very important to share with you.

I spent years and years teaching weekend survival courses (roughly 30 attendees each weekend) and selling survival products through various platforms, including online and live events. I built a great little business around this model, but I was always hustling to sell the next product and fill the next course. It NEVER felt easy. Teaching LIVE courses in the field was A TON of work (more than most realize), and selling products required keeping inventory, as well as packaging and shipping them to the customer. If I would have built my in-house email list early on, this entire model would have been much easier. I could have on-ramped customers and introduced them to my host of products and services and kept in touch with them over time with special promotions, tips, tricks, and teachings. I could have drastically increased the LIFETIME VALUE of a customer.

Making your FIRST SALE to a customer will always be your hardest and most expensive one. It is absolutely VITAL that you do everything within your power in increase the LIFETIME VALUE of that customer by selling them more products and services over the course of the coming weeks, months, and even years. It is an IN-HOUSE email list that will allow you to do this!

CHAPTER 10

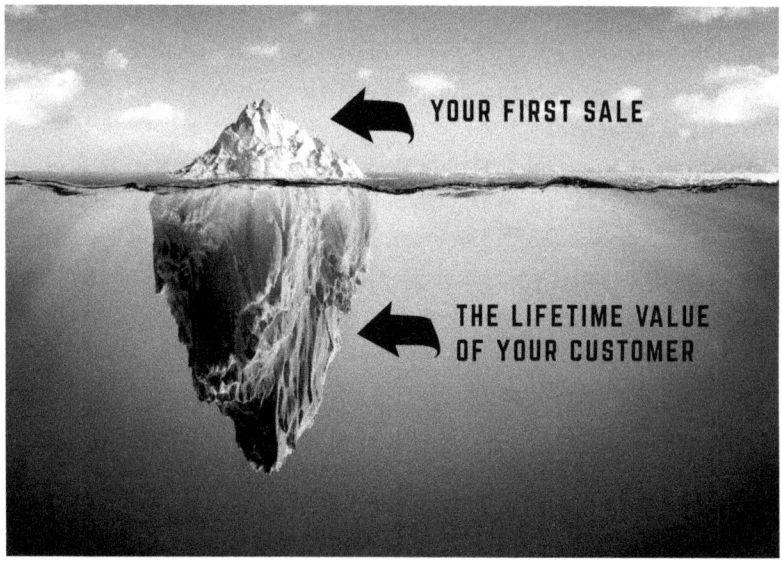

I want to take a moment to tell you about something that changed my business forever. One of the biggest hurdles when teaching live survival courses was that people had to travel to my training facility. This DRASTICALLY impacted my reach. I was also limited by the time of year. AND, I could only handle roughly 30 students per course. There were limitations all over the place. And, quite frankly, after doing this for 15 years, I started to realize that if I didn't change anything, then I was going to be doing the same thing when I'm 80, with the same limitations. If I was tired in my late 30s, I was going to be unimaginably tired in my 80s! If truth be told, I wanted to work less and make more.

So, I started to think about my business differently. I wanted to AUTOMATE my business so that I didn't have to work so hard and so long. This is what really led me to build my email list and develop the on-ramp process I've discussed with you. It became a SYSTEM that I could use to introduce customers to my products and services—automatically. This process helped to fill LIVE events and sell more products, but it didn't really

CHAPTER 10

help with the other limitations I mentioned. People still had to travel. I was still limited by the time of year. I could only teach a small number of students at a time. Doing courses every weekend was A LOT OF WORK! Maybe you can relate?

So, one day, I asked myself, "I wonder if I could teach these skills through an online course?" This would allow me to teach as many people as I wanted, no matter where they lived in the world. We wouldn't be in the woods, but I could show them everything in the comfort of their own homes, and I could charge a fraction of the price. I would teach the same skills, just in a different way, and over the internet.

I had decided earlier in my career that survival skills couldn't be taught online and that people only came to courses because they wanted to get outside. Two years went by, and I was still in the same rut and week-to-week grind.

Meanwhile, online education EXPLODED and the technology for teaching online courses became easier and easier to use and navigate. Finally, I broke down and decided to build my first online survival course. Hesitantly, I emailed my list of customers—worried about what they would think about learning survival skills online—and (almost instantly) had the LARGEST SINGLE SALES DAY of my entire survival career. I sold almost $24,000 worth of an $89 course the first day and another $10,000 of that same course with a follow-up email to my list the second day. I was blown away by the response. People LOVED the idea. They LOVED that they could learn these skills from home. They LOVED that they didn't have to travel. They LOVED that the cost was easily affordable. They LOVED that they could watch the course around their own schedule. To date, it was the most successful product launch in my business.

CHAPTER 10

First day sales stats after launching my first online course
(Art of Fire) to my in-house email list.

As much as I loved having that big sales day, you want to know what I love even more? Now that I'm done filming that course, I can continue to sell it and deliver it digitally online, 24/7, without having to do a single thing. I immediately added that course to my automated customer on-ramp email series and now sell a handful of them every single week. This year, I'll make almost $30,000 of completely passive income from JUST THAT ONE SINGLE COURSE, and it's all sold and delivered AUTOMATICALLY for me. I sometimes have to pinch myself. These are JUST THE SALES from new customers who enter my automated on-ramp email process.

Imagine what it would feel like to add $30,000/year of passive income to your bottom line just by adding in one single automated email?

Two years ago, I would have thought that was impossible! The best part is that it involves doing exactly what I love—sharing survival skills with other people.

This is only possible because I have a system in place that:

1. Attracts my ideal customer

2. Collects their email

3. And automatically takes them on a sales journey

CHAPTER 10

This concept was a game changer for me, and I believe it can be a game changer for you and your business, too! If you are building your business around your own area of expertise, I believe that one of the best and most salable products you can offer your potential customers is an online course of some kind that showcases your gifts, skills, and talents by SOLVING A PROBLEM FOR THEM or TEACHING THEM SOMETHING. The online learning business is already claiming BILLIONS of dollars annually, and it is growing like gangbusters! You can offer your customer AN INSANE amount of value through an online course. Online courses ARE NOT just for technology-based businesses. I'm using them right now to teach survival skills (of all things)! I guarantee that you can also teach your outdoor-related skill in an online course! I even sell a course about how to process and eat acorns. It's DOES NOT get more obscure than that!

When someone signs up for one of my online courses, I consider that a "GATEWAY PRODUCT." This is a way for someone to train with me without too much commitment. Once they sign up, they become a part of my world, and I offer them other products and services related to that course, including a LIVE training at my facility for a PREMIUM price. Even though my course may only cost $50, I always try to increase the lifetime value of that customer by continuing to offer them related products, services, or courses. I do this all automatically through automated email campaigns that I set up only once. This is all very similar to what I've already discussed with you.

These days, I spend much more time running my business than my business running me! I also spend much less time doing things that feel like work. It wasn't until recently that the technology was available for this concept to even be a reality, and I could have never even dreamt of making it happen without putting into action the 5 PILLARS of my SURVIVAL CEO 5-PILLAR BLUEPRINT that I've shared with you in this book.

CHAPTER 10

YOUR INVITATION TO OUTDOORCORE.COM

If you possess an outdoor-related skill, whether it be in survival, rock climbing, kayaking, fishing, basketry, wild edibles, or anything else, I'd like to invite you to an online course platform that my team and I have developed exclusively for outdoor skills teachers and seekers called **http://www.outdoorcore.com.**

OutdoorCore.com is an online teaching platform that connects outdoor teachers with outdoor seekers and makes getting your first salable course off the ground very easy.

Even if you have other products and services, an online course is a perfect product to integrate into your customer on-ramp email series. Online courses can be an amazing revenue stream IN ADDITION to the products and services that you already offer or plan to offer. Remember, you make it only once and can sell it forever! In the world of business—this is a thing of pure magic.

The great thing about being an instructor at OutdoorCore.com is sharing traffic with other instructors, LIKE MYSELF, who are driving customers to the platform.

CHAPTER 10

It took me years to get an online course up and running. Now, with OutdoorCore.com, you can have an online course up and running in less than a week and have INSTANT traffic. Then, you can integrate that course into your own SURVIVAL CEO 5-PILLAR BLUEPRINT that we've discussed and have an almost IMMEDIATE salable product that is essentially pure profit.

CHAPTER 11: BUILDING YOUR 5 PILLARS WITH EXPERT INSTRUCTION

But Creek—you have a television show—you're rich!!!!

You have no idea how much I hear that from people. My family and I laugh out loud at that statement. In fact, let me put it to you this way: If it wasn't for the SURVIVAL CEO 5-PILLAR BLUEPRINT that I've outlined in this book to help me grow my business, I wouldn't even be able to afford to the take the time off work to film a television show. It is my BUSINESS that allows me to pursue ANY television project I've worked on to date. Contrary to what 99% of people believe, there is VERY LITTLE money to be made in most reality television, especially in the beginning.

Yes, the television programs I've been involved with have been great for marketing, but without an automatic system in place to capture leads and take them through an on-ramp process, then no amount of marketing in the world would have made a difference. Trust me, I know tons of people who have been on TV and have nothing to show for it. That's because they don't have a system in place to drive business on the back end. The same is true for ANY other kind of marketing effort, including magazine ads, news appearances, books, tradeshows, direct mail, flyers, Facebook ads, Google AdWords, BLOG articles, and the list goes on. If a system like I've described in this book is not in place, **YOU ARE MISSING OUT ON A HUGE OPPORTUNITY TO BUILD YOUR EMAIL LIST AND GROW YOUR BUSINESS AND BRAND!** It doesn't matter whether you have 2 people or 2,000 visiting your platform each day, this system should be a foundation for building your online business.

IF A SYSTEM LIKE I'VE DESCRIBED IN THIS BOOK IS NOT IN PLACE, **YOU ARE MISSING OUT ON A HUGE OPPORTUNITY TO BUILD YOUR EMAIL LIST AND GROW YOUR BUSINESS AND BRAND!**

CHAPTER 11

I can't tell you how many people I've met who have had incredible exposure on television, through magazine articles, YouTube, or online platforms, yet they DO NOT have a system in place to help them MONETIZE that exposure. It's sad and such a missed opportunity. If you know someone in this position—PLEASE GIVE THEM A COPY OF THIS BOOK!

It literally makes me sick to my stomach when I watch a great teacher give all their hard-earned knowledge away on YouTube in hopes that someday YouTube will pay them a few dollars for views. My goal with this book is to tell you THERE IS A BETTER WAY TO MAKE MONEY WITH YOUR KNOWLEDGE!

It took me over 15 years to figure out a system that was able to convert my very obscure business in the wilderness survival space into a REAL FULL-TIME BUSINESS that could provide for me and my family. Not only did I not understand the concepts that I've outlined for you in this book, but the technology wasn't there to support it. Right now, YOU are in a much different position than I was.

I want to quickly revisit the 4 principles I learned while cutting hair in my college dormitory:

1. Give them something of VALUE for FREE

2. Get their contact information

3. Build a relationship with your customer

4. Try to get them to come back for more (and hopefully buy something)

I've used these same principles to build my wilderness survival business, and I'm convinced that you can use them to build your own business, no matter how obscure it may be. Below are the main steps to my **SURVIVAL CEO 5-PILLAR BLUEPRINT:**

CHAPTER 11

1. **CREATE KILLER CONTENT** (using a blog or other online platform, such as YouTube)
2. When people view content, make an offer to GIVE them something of VALUE for FREE.
3. Get their email address.
4. Convert them from COLD to WARM traffic (build a relationship) using an automated email campaign (webinars can also be used here).
5. Make them an offer for a product or service within my business.
6. Try to get them to come back for more by continuing to offer them VALUE and keeping in touch with them through regular email updates.
7. In recent years, I've taken this a step further and now ASK my email list WHAT PRODUCTS they want me to create for them!

I don't care what your business is, this formula can transform it or help you get it off the ground. I am living proof. Contrary to what many people believe (because of my television presence), I do not have a team of marketing professionals working behind the scenes. I AM THE MARKETING DEPARTMENT at Creek, Inc. You do not need to hire someone to do this for you. You can totally do it yourself, no matter where you're at in your business right now—even if you don't have tech skills or money.

FREE 1-HOUR TRAINING

If you haven't already, please watch my FREE 1-Hour Training that serves as an excellent supplement to this book.

In the training, I dig deeper into how to implement my SURVIVAL CEO 5 PILLAR BLUEPRINT SYSTEM into your own brand and business. In this video training, I show you examples I use in my own businesses to help it make even more sense. If you haven't already seen it, you can watch it RIGHT NOW at: **http://www.survivalceo.com/free-training**

I believe that this training will greatly help you in putting together all the pieces I've described in this book, within your own brand and business.

THE SURVIVAL CEO 5-PILLAR BLUEPRINT ONLINE COURSE

At this point, you either believe this strategy could help your business or not. You're either ready to start implementing something similar on your own or not. Either way, it's fine by me. My goal was to show what has worked for me and what's possible. That was my promise at the beginning of this book, and I believe I've delivered on that promise.

Right now, I want you to imagine that you are at a fork in the road.

One direction leads to you starting to implement all the parts and pieces of the process I've just outlined—by yourself. I know that you can absolutely do it on your own, using this guide as a reference. It will take self-discipline and hard work, but you can do it!

However, you and I both know that the fastest path to get where you want to be is by working directly with someone who has been there and done that. We also both know that the devil is in the details. While I've covered **A LOT** of information in this book, there are many critical details that didn't make it onto these pages.

The other fork in the road leads you to an online course where you work one-on-one with me to help you implement this entire process into your business, in just 30-minutes a day, over the course of a few weeks. I'll teach you, one-on-one, exactly how to do all of it within your own business. I literally open the doors to the back end of my business and teach you. Whether you have an existing business or blog or nothing at all, I take you by the hand from the very beginning and walk you through every step of the process.

CHAPTER 11

The time, effort, and the money you'll save will be IMMEASURABLE.

Most people who try to do it on their own never actually do because the process can be overwhelming, and they have no one to keep them accountable. Also, you're just not as committed to something that you don't pay for. I've learned that the hard way.

The quicker you get this done, the quicker you can start building your business into what you know it can be, and the quicker you can start making an impact in the lives of the people who are already trying to find you and the solutions or products that you have for them!

I teach everything on video, while you look over my shoulder at my computer screen—INSIDE of my business.

YOU NEED TO KNOW THIS

It's important that you know that I make, BY FAR, the bulk of my income from my WILDERNESS SURVIVAL BUSINESS. This is the HOBBY that I converted into a REAL CAREER.

Why do you need to know this?

You should always be leery of taking (or purchasing) business advice from someone who's ONLY made their money in selling business advice. This is a recipe for a SCAM. I've made (and make) my living as a WILDERNESS SURVIVAL INSTRUCTOR. This is what I LOVE to do. I've been able to do this because of the system that I've developed. This SYSTEM is a skill that I've honed over many years, through starting multiple businesses, much like my fire-starting skills. I use it EVERY DAY and KNOW that it works.

Bottom line—never buy business lessons from a person who has never had a business doing anything outside of selling business lessons!

CHAPTER 11

No matter where you are at right now and no matter what business you hope to start, by the end of my online SURVIVAL CEO 5 PILLAR BLUEPRINT ONLINE COURSE, you will have the following foundational marketing PILLARS in place:

PILLAR # 1: YOUR PLATFORM

You'll choose and build out your own platform and blog space (if you don't already have one) to serve as a hub for your content and email list building efforts. You'll create the key webpages you need and set everything up for success.

PILLAR # 2: YOUR CONTENT

You'll understand the RIGHT WAY to build content that attracts your perfect audience. CONTENT IS KING! You'll learn exactly how to choose topics that your ideal customer is already searching for. You'll write your own blog posts according to my proven BLOG POST TEMPLATE. We will cover all of the important SEO tactics so that you'll quickly rank with Google. You'll TWICE BAKE your content to create valuable Lead Magnets and multipurpose your content on social media and other platforms to get more traffic! I walk you through every step of the process with video tutorials, step-by-step instructions, and fill-in-the-blank templates.

PILLAR # 3: YOUR TRAFFIC

You'll understand how to generate FREE BUT NOT FREE traffic. It will require work, but I'll save you a ton of time (and money). You'll master my secrets that GET RESULTS. We attack guest blog posting, Pinterest, YouTube strategies, Facebook Group Marketing and several other hidden gems. You'll master each one, step-by-step, and apply them to your CONTENT and business right now! I'll give you my TRAFFIC CHECKLISTS to make it super simple, so you don't miss a single step in the process. Just follow my Traffic Formula and watch the stats start to climb!

PILLAR # 4: YOUR EMAIL LIST

You'll start to BUILD your in-house email list—the lifeblood of your business—like a seasoned pro. We will make sure you have everything in place to capture emails. You'll integrate all the moving pieces, learn how to build successful Lead Magnets, and integrate them strategically into your business. I'll help you develop your PDF downloads, your online challenges, your checklists, your free videos, and any other Lead Magnet you wish to use. I'll show you the ones I use to build my own list and how to copy them for your own business. You will become an email-list-building MONSTER! I want you to live and breathe EMAIL LIST BUILDING. Your email list is your most valuable business asset! Remember, your income will be directly proportional to the size of your email list. Get ready to grow both!

PILLAR # 5: YOUR CUSTOMER ON-RAMP

You'll begin turning cold leads into warm prospects. You'll use my tried and true process (and fill-in-the-blank templates) for writing email on-ramps. These templates alone are worth the price of the course! I take all of the guess work out of the process for you—just follow my Customer On-Ramp Formula!

In addition to making sure your 5 MARKETING PILLARS are in place and working properly, you'll be part of my SURVIVAL CEO TRIBE. This is a closed community of like-minded entrepreneurs who share ideas, success, failures, and questions that relate to business marketing as they relate to the SURVIVAL CEO 5-PILLAR BLUEPRINT. The value of this community is immeasurable. I will also be there to answer any questions you have and help you overcome hurdles. You'll also have access to my monthly LIVE coaching calls where I discuss topical updates and answer questions you and other students might have.

If you've followed what I do for very long, you know that my passion in life is teaching people. That's why I still love holding survival courses—because I love working with and teaching people skills that can impact their life. The same is true with the business-building information I've shared with you in this book.

If you haven't figured it out yet, THIS BOOK is my LEAD MAGNET. I got up at 5am every morning for 3 months to write this book. I wrote from 5–7am every day (seven days a week) for 3 months to create this LEAD MAGNET for you. Most people aren't willing to put in that kind of effort. Regardless of what I charge for this book, it's worth thousands of dollars to the right person. To the person who takes this stuff to the next level, it's priceless. It is my sincere hope that this book, in some way, shape, or form, helps you to grow your business or get your idea off the ground—or better yet—helps you to turn your passion into an actual money-making venture for you and your family. There are few realized dreams better than this!

Have you been scratching your head trying to get your idea off the ground or take your existing business to the next level? If so, I want to ask you two questions:

1. If you don't take action NOW, when will you?

2. If you don't work with ME, who else do you know and trust to (or even CAN) teach you how to implement a proven business building system?

You have absolutely nothing to lose. As with my Wilderness Survival Business, everything I offer has a 100% money back (no questions asked) satisfaction guarantee. If you take my course and you aren't getting the result you hoped for, then I'll refund all of your money.

CHAPTER 11

I really hope to see you on the inside of the SURVIVAL CEO 5-PILLAR BLUEPRINT COURSE soon so that we can transfer all I know to your own business, dreams, and ideas!

Everyone deserves to do what they LOVE for a living—that includes you!

Get started right now at: **http://www.survivalceo.com/course**

CHAPTER 12: THE WRAP-UP

Whether I'm teaching someone about survival skills or how I've built my Wilderness Survival business into a small empire, the result is the same. My goal is to help others become more self-reliant. Self-reliance must run in my veins. If you've picked up this book, it must run in yours, too. That makes us "like-minded" in some respects. I hope to continue to train with you in one way or another!

Whether you opt-in for my SURVIVAL CEO 5-PILLAR BLUEPRINT Online Course or not, it is truly my prayer that something I've shared with you here makes a difference in taking your business or business idea to the next level. If I can carve out a business for myself in the odd-ball wilderness survival space, then I know you can do it in your Smitch Niche, too—whatever that may be! If something I've taught you in this book does help you, please let me know—I'd love to hear about it. You can email me directly at creek@creekstewart.com.

I always think it's a good idea to give a TO DO list at the end of an instructional book. So, if you want to implement some of the things I've discussed here on your own, below is your CHECKLIST:

- ❏ Choose a PLATFORM where you will be releasing CONTENT (in my opinion it should be a BLOG, but other options include FACEBOOK, INSTAGRAM, and YOUTUBE).
- ❏ Start developing content and posting it! Post at least 1 new piece of content (if using a blog) per week. Be sure to do your research and MAKE SURE you're creating content that your target market is already searching for.
- ❏ Decide what your LEAD MAGNET will be. What is the piece of

CHAPTER 12

FREE and VALUABLE information you'll be giving away in exchange for a visitor's email address?

❏ Create your LEAD MAGNET.

❏ Start an account with either MailChimp or ActiveCampaign so that you can collect emails and start creating an automated ON-RAMP CAMPAIGN for potential customers.

❏ Write your automated email on-ramp campaign.

❏ Make the integrations between your place of content (i.e., blog) and your marketing email software.

❏ Begin seeking out GUEST POSTING opportunities (to grow your reach and drive free TRAFFIC).

❏ Begin possible publicity campaigns (to grow your reach and drive traffic).

❏ Share BLOG posts on social media & PINTEREST.

❏ Offer your LEAD MAGNET in ALL your YouTube videos.

❏ Consider building a 5-day challenge as one of your LEAD MAGNETS.

❏ Continue to develop SEO DRIVEN KILLER CONTENT.

❏ Ask your customers what PRODUCTS & SERVICES they WANT from you!

❏ Sell them THOSE products!

❏ Trust the Process.

If you haven't already, be sure to check out my Facebook page, titled SURVIVAL CEO, at this link: https://www.facebook.com/survivalceo/ I'll be using it as a hub to discuss topics related to tips, tricks, and strategies for building a viable business around your outdoor passion. I'll also be available to answer any questions you have about the content that I've offered in this book or in my online business-related video tutorials and courses. Also, on the following pages, I've listed a few of the resources that I use most often to execute many of the strategies detailed in this book.

And, for goodness sake—make sure you're ON MY EMAIL LIST (SURVIVALCEO.COM/LIST)!!!

Remember, it's not IF but WHEN,

RESOURCE LIST

CREEK'S RESOURCE LIST

RESOURCES USED TO CREATE LEAD MAGNETS

Microsoft Word: Many simple downloadable templates, such as checklists, can be created in Microsoft Word and virtually printed as a PDF. This PDF can be used as the FREE DOWNLOAD.

http://www.fiverr.com: I use FIVERR quite a bit to hire design help. If you want to create a downloadable (or even print) book that is a little more polished and professional than what you can do yourself in Microsoft Word, then FIVERR is your place. There are TONS of people on FIVERR who do design work for very reasonable prices. For booklet layout, click GRAPHICS & DESIGN, then click FLYERS & BROCHURES. Of course, you can use FIVERR for logos, web graphics, and pretty much anything you can image designed as well.

MARKETING EMAIL PROVIDERS

http://www.activecampaign.com : ActiveCampaign is the email marketing platform that I use to house all of my email lists and manage my automated email campaigns. It's awesome and I love it. I started using MailChimp (highlighted below) but switched over to ActiveCampaign because I felt like it was a little more robust at the time (although MailChimp has made some great upgrades recently).

http://www.mailchimp.com: I used MailChimp to manage all of my email lists for a long time and really liked it. It is very user friendly and affordable. Initially, I used it because they had a FREE plan and I was broke. MailChimp is a great option and has made some big upgrades to their service offerings in the past couple of years.

WEBSITE HOSTING:

http://www.godaddy.com: I use GoDaddy for all my website hosting. Every time I call the phone number, a real human picks up and that goes a LONG way. They also make it very easy to integrate within most every other service I use.

WEBSITE BUILDING PLATFORM:

http://www.wordpress.net: I started my first blog, willowhavenoutdoor.com, on WordPress and it's still hosted there today. WordPress is the most popular blogging platform. There are 1000s of very professional templates to choose from, and setting it up with GoDaddy is very easy to do. Just call GoDaddy and they will walk you through the process.

http://www.squarespace.com: Many of my websites are built and hosted on SquareSpace. Despite how it might seem, I'm not a techie and SquareSpace is very user friendly. I can build a very professional looking website with SquareSpace in just a few hours. My main site, http://www.creekstewart.com, is built and hosted on SquareSpace. Also, connecting it to GoDaddy (so you can have your own domain name) is as simple as clicking a button inside of your SquareSpace dashboard.

CPSIA information can be obtained
at www.ICGtesting.com
Printed in the USA
FSHW022132230420